Three-Week SAT Crash Course - Reading

FIRST EDITION

ISBN: 978-0-9992711-1-7
Library of Congress Control Number: 2021905143

www.VohraMethod.com

Table of Contents

What if I have more than Three Weeks?

Wait Chelsey! What should I do if I have more than three weeks before my test? Should I just wait around until three weeks before and then start this training?

No. First of all, don't be dumb. That would be very, very stupid. Please do not do that. In fact, don't even wait for ONE DAY. Get started today.

Second, if you have more than three weeks, you should read this book, and then follow the additional training suggestions at the end of the book. The additional training can continue for however much time you have available. It just gets harder and harder until you can surpass any obstacle and you're nearly guaranteeing yourself a perfect score.

If you want a fast score boost, this book can get you there in three weeks. If you want a perfect score, the additional training will get you there in three months or more. You have to DO it, and you have to pour your heart and soul and everything into it. You should spend a lot of time on this training regardless. But, it can be done!

So, don't wait ever. Avoidance will never get you a good SAT score. Other obligations will never get you a good SAT score. Your friend's birthday party, your next three soccer matches, your piano practice, and your great aunt and uncle's wedding anniversary...will all NOT get you a good score. So, get your priorities straight and get down to business!

How to Improve Your SAT Reading Score in Three Weeks

Read this book. Do the things the book tells you to do. Actually do them! Don't just pretend or say that you'll do it later and then forget. Answer every question yourself. Find every piece of evidence. Take all the time it takes now so that you can be fast and reliable when you take the real test.

Accuracy comes first; speed comes second.

If you need help, contact me at VohraMethod.com or CSnyder@VohraMethod.com.

Free Vocabulary Building Software and a few quick facts about the SAT

I'm going to assume, because you're reading this, that you already:

1. Think the SAT is important.
2. Want to get a perfect (or very high score).
3. Realize that the SAT is a serious challenge.
4. Want your SAT training to take as little time as possible.

I won't waste time convincing you of the above. But, I do want to add something to point number 2.

The SAT is a very formidable opponent.

This is more than a fact; it's a call to action. You must fundamentally change the way you think about the SAT if you want to get a perfect score. **First**, from this point forward, you must never utter the words, "Oh, I just made a simple mistake."

There are no "simple mistakes" on the SAT. There are just people who get paid to come up with new ways to make you get stuff wrong on the SAT...and you fell for it.

There are also no "guessing methods", and there is no such thing as "two correct answer choices, but one of them is better". All of that is nonsense, and you must get it out of your brain immediately. Those thoughts will guarantee that you **don't** get a perfect score.

Second, you must immediately throw your calculator off a balcony, into the trash, or into the backpack of your worst enemy. Calculators will make you exactly the kind of button-punching monkey that can only achieve mediocrity on the SAT.

"Quickly trying out all the answers" is not an approach that will work for a perfect score, or even a 1500+. It's just slow nonsense that will create more stress as it eats up all your time. Even worse, it indicates that there is some fundamental piece of Algebra that you don't know. You can't just let yourself not know those pieces of Algebra. You must fill in those gaps quickly and permanently. Then, you won't need a calculator anyways.

Start good mental habits right away.

Your First Good Habit: Study Vocabulary every day!

If you already have a system for studying vocabulary, use that. If you don't, we'll get you set up with our Vocabulary Synapse software that we offer to everyone completely free because we know how important vocabulary is to your success.

Several questions on the SAT directly test your vocabulary knowledge. BUT! They almost always pick a word with multiple meanings...and then list ALL those meanings as your four answer choices.

Alternatively, they will just pick a word that's hard and you either know it or you don't.

Several other questions on the SAT indirectly test your vocabulary by requiring evidence that has dense vocabulary in it. If you don't understand that sentence in the passage, you're going to get the question AND the evidence question wrong. And it was all an issue of vocab...

Vocab is important. It's also easy to study with our free Vocab Synapse program.

Set up a free consultation today at www.VohraMethod.com and we'll get you set up with access to your daily vocab training.

Study vocabulary every single day.

Your Second Good Habit: Laughter

In order to do well on the SAT, the number one thing you need is someone to look at the mistakes you've made and jovially laugh at you.

But Chelsey, getting laughed at doesn't sound fun...

Well, taking the SAT isn't a party either. The point is that you don't just need to be told what you did wrong. You need to get into a place where you can laugh at yourself for the ridiculous answers and mistakes you're making. Only then will you really change.

If you can't afford a private tutor, just laugh at yourself when you mess up. If you can, come work with me.

Laughter is also uplifting and healing. You don't need to wallow in the grief of your first SAT attempt, or your first practice test score. You need to overcome that first score. Laughter is a positive way to train the brain to stop making lazy, ridiculous errors.

Final Note: Most students come into our courses and our private sessions carrying a lot of emotional baggage. "I'm terrible at tests." "I always do poorly on the math section." "My parents and I have been fighting about this stupid test for months."

Whatever your emotional baggage is, put it on the next flight to Mars and don't look back. Everything you've done so far, all the worrying and bickering and wallowing and nonsense, got you to where you are now. If you don't want to stay where you are now, then you need to do something different.

Learn Your Tactics & Rules

If you have three weeks.

If you have three weeks until your test, and you don't really feel ready... reschedule your test. I would like to point out that this is the most obvious solution, and yet nearly every family I've worked with for over 7 years looks at me like I have 12 heads when I suggest it.

If you're not ready, then you're not ready. There is no magic that can make you ready. The SAT isn't a test of magic, so don't kid yourself. It's a test of raw knowledge (for math and grammar) and of skill (in all three subjects).

However, if the test three weeks from now (roughly) is your absolute last opportunity to improve your score, then you have a lot of work to do, which is the point of this book.

(**Important Note:** The last possible test you can take for early admissions for colleges is actually usually the December test. The latest possible test for regular decision is also December, as there is no test in January.

There is a HUGE difference between the last possible test you can take and the last time you feel like taking the test. Your SAT score will matter more than your school GPA, and most of your charitable work and extracurriculars. Don't be a lazy dumb-o. Take the test again until you get the score that will secure you the future you deserve.)

We'll start with the general tactics and rules.

Tactic 1: The SRS

You need to make the SAT reading passages more SIMPLE, not more complex!

Good grief, if I told you some of the crazy, convoluted, mental-gymnastics-style answers I've gotten to the simplest of questions...well, hopefully we would share a good laugh.

You know if you're a student who does this. When asked a question in English class, 40% of your answer is just an elaborate and circuitous rephrasing of the question, followed by an elaborate and circuitous re-ordering of so many words from the passage that it sort of sounds like you know what you're saying. In reality, you're just making a Frankenstein monster out of the passage, hoping that the more complex and unreadable your answer looks (boy do you LOVE the thesaurus!) the better your grade will be.

Now, here's the kicker.

The more you made your answers complex and unreadable and full of 15 letter synonyms for simple words...the better your grades got!!

I've always said that high school in America these days doesn't teach you much, and most of it you forget with just a little break, but the one skill high schools across the nation never fail to teach is how to bullshit.

My point is this: It's not your fault. Literally NONE of your current SAT situation is your fault. Your whole life, people told you, "If you do this, you'll be smart." "If you do this, you'll get into a good college." "If you do this, you'll get a good job, make good money, and have a good life."

I won't get into all the flaws in those statements. You're probably already waking up to the harsh reality of college admissions.

The point is, those people lied to you. Everything they made you do did NOT prepare you for what, in reality, is a pretty basic test of Algebra, English grammar, and critical reading.

It's not your fault that you're starting where you are. But, after reading this book, your next score will be your fault (**and your own proud achievement**).

How do we combat what your school has taught you for 13 years (or so)?

It's actually pretty simple, but it will probably be physically painful at first. You have to create the Simple, Ridiculous Summary (the SRS).

But Chelsey, I've done summaries before. That doesn't sound too bad!

Well, there's a twist. The most important rule of the SRS is that you specifically MUST make your English teacher cry. If your English teacher read this summary, not only would she give you an F-, she would also immediately burst into tears!

Why?

Because, your school taught you how to read in such a convoluted way that you can't even answer a simple question simply! So, whatever your school thinks is a "simple" summary...it ain't.

And how do we create this SRS?

Easy, use English bad.

If there's a passage about scientists who are studying the activity of a particular volcano, and they don't know why this one volcano erupted so much earlier than anticipated, and they want to use that information to create a model for other, less predictable volcanoes...then you write, "Earth made a surprise 'splosion and scientists be like, what it do?!"

Use crazy words like ain't, gon' (meaning going to), fam, lit...

Use silly phrases like 'what it do' and 'up in here' and 'be like'. One of my favorites is "ain't nobody got time for that."

The point is to make your summary chill. The way you would describe a book to your bros or your gals.

Ain't nobody up in here like, "My dearest compatriot. Thineself shouldst peruse Twilight, a new text which encompasses the woes of a teenaged female attempting to procure for herself an interest of endearment who is neither a homo sapiens nor a matte-skinned fellow."

You guys have got to loosen up... I hope at this point you're having a good laugh at yourself, because I definitely am!

So, here are the specific requirements:

How to write the SRS (Simple, Ridiculous Summary)

1. You must use the phrase "**be like**". (It basically means "says" or "thinks".)
2. You must use **no more than two sentences**.
3. Your summary must be **comprehensible to a 5-year-old**.
4. Your summary **must NOT include any of the words from the passage**.

So, make it ridiculous. Use crazy phrases. Keep it very short (as short as possible, only 1 sentence is perfectly acceptable). Really boil the ideas down. Everything can be explained, on some level, to a 5-year-old. You can make it that simple, and you should. And whatever you do, don't just pull 50 words from the passage, stick them in a hat, jumble them up, and spit them back out as some kind of pseudo-intelligence. We will have none of that!

How to Use Your SRS:

After you practice with this skill a bit (practice exercises will come at the end of this chapter), you'll be wondering, "but, how does this help me?"

First, there is very often a question on at least 3 of the 5 SAT passages that will directly ask you for a summary. It might ask for a summary of just the first paragraph. It might ask something like, "How does the passage progress?" You'll often see questions asking about the main idea. All of these things will relate back to your simple summary.

But then, there will be questions you wouldn't expect that will lean heavily into just a basic, surface level understanding of the passage. This is especially true in the fiction passages, where emotions and human motivations are key. Things like deception, too, would stand out in your SRS. And, if your SRS is good, then you'll find one answer choice clearly describing whatever deception or intention or desire you pinpointed. It's hard to spot at first, but you can get it with practice.

You'll find a specific, partnered exercise on this later in the chapter. Just keep this mantra in mind: When in doubt, go back to your Simple, Ridiculous Summary.

How to Practice:

First, you WILL need practice on this. Everything above sounds so simple (if a bit silly); I know. But, every student I have worked with **always** immediately reverts back to his/her old ways. It takes about 10 seconds for students to give me summaries that are 150-word-long run-on sentences, or just 8 sentences long, or contain entire 20-word QUOTES from the passage! And it takes everyone a while to get used to the physical uncomfortableness of using bad English when you think you're supposed to be studying English.

I get it; this is weird. It's weird, and it works. I've helped students improve their reading scores by 120+ points in 6 hours of tutoring. If you're looking for a "magic spell" that will get you an amazing score very, very fast...this is the closest thing you'll find.

But, you have to commit to it. You have to actually follow the requirements for the SRS. You have to actually make a SRS for every passage. You need to practice.

If you want to practice with SAT passages, you really need some external person to rigorously tell you if your SRS is too complex, too short-sighted, too long, etc. If you want to work with me, you can visit VohraMethod.com. Otherwise, find the most renegade person you know and show them the requirements, then show them your summary attempts.

You can't use your teachers; they'll just tell you that your English is bad, and they'll start crying (that's the point!). You can't use your parents (sorry mom and dad) because they will also be very off-put by the poor English and silly phrases. If, by chance, your mom or dad is super renegade, then use them.

You need someone who reads a lot, and who isn't afraid to break the rules. The "rules" of your life have been that if you put out terrible summaries that are basically longer than the passage and equally as dense, then you win. On the SAT, you do that...you lose.

Exercise: Rely on the SRS

1. Get a partner. Pick someone who is smart, has read this book, and is trying to get a perfect SAT score (no slackers allowed!).
2. Get a Barron's SAT book with practice tests. DO NOT use the official College Board tests for this! Those are limited, and you need them for your official practice.
3. Pick out two fiction passages. These will come from two separate tests. You take one; your partner takes one.
4. Both of you read your passage and make your best SRS.
5. Give your partner the questions from your passage (which he/she has not read), and also pass over your SRS. Your partner will now attempt to answer as many questions as possible using ONLY the SRS (no reading the passage!). You do the same with your partner's passage.
6. Don't expect to get all of the questions right, obviously. But, you will get SOME of them right. This is very powerful, and it will help you build up the right intuition to dominate the SAT.
7. Repeat this exercise for each passage type. You should both do science passages at the same time, dual passages at the same time, etc.

Basically, practice as much as you possibly can until your test date. The SAT will matter more than almost anything else you put in your college application. If you're trying to get recruited for a sport, your SAT score will matter about 100 times more than all school grades, extracurriculars, and college essays combined because they need to keep their SAT averages up for the team as a whole.

Just keep practicing and don't stop until your test day. If you can't find a partner, you can come hang out with me. You can also practice your SRS on books that you read for fun, on news articles and journals, on anything.

Tactic 2: Focus Your Attention

This rule will be a bit quicker, and also passage specific.

Fiction Passages

If you read enough of the fiction passages on the SAT, you'll slowly realize that...there are almost no actions that ever happen!

Seriously, the characters don't DO anything. If they do, they do like ONE thing. The passages are like the following:

» A dude walks home and thinks a lot of thoughts.
» A guy shows up at someone's house and worries about the brief conversation they have.
» A guy ponders why he is going on a trip, and at some point the wind blows.

I'm not making these up, by the way. Those are all from real SAT passages (bonus points if you can figure out which ones!).

In those passages, the actions are:

» Walking
» Showing up at a house AND having a conversation (this one has a LOT of action, lol)
» Wind blowing

This is actually one reason why many students end up not enjoying literary fiction very much. Literary fiction is all about thinking, and thinking about thinking, and the thought of thinking about thoughts someone once had while thinking. (Okay, I joke, but it's sort of true.)

Don't get me wrong, I'm a bigger literary fiction nerd than most. And, I think it's really important to analyze the way other people think. You'll only meet so many people in real life, and of those people, many will have roughly the same thoughts. But, in books, the characters are often quite diverse. Authors specifically try to make uncommon characters, because that is obviously more interesting. That means that you get to see very weird nuances of humanity, and that's important no matter where you want your life to go.

That said, reading about a lot of thoughts can get a little droll.

Side Tip #1: Fake it til you feel it. I always tell my students to just pretend that the passages are super interesting. If you're suffering through a passage, you'll almost certainly miss 5 questions on that one passage. I see it constantly. But, if you laugh a little, or just force yourself to smile and pretend it's sort of interesting, you'll usually do a lot better. (This is another reason why the Simple, Ridiculous Summary is so useful!)

Okay, that was a lot of intro, now here's the main point:

In fiction passages, you should focus on the ACTIONS.

If anything actually happens in a fiction passage, you can bet that there will be a question pertaining to that action. There might even be 2 or 3 questions that relate to that action. Remember, the SRS covered 1-2 questions already. So, another 2-3 can get you close to halfway through the fiction passage, and that's just with TWO rules so far.

How do you use this?

Normally, I encourage students to laugh at themselves for their ridiculous <u>underlining</u> habits. So many students come to me enthusiastically proclaiming that they absolutely LOVE annotating the text.

Guess who taught you how to annotate? Yep. Your schools.

So, I look at the "annotations" and what do I see? About 98% of the passage is underlined. Well, if that's what you want, I can just type up every SAT passage, select all, and ctrl + U for you!

Obviously, this annotation "tactic" is completely useless and pretty much just nonsense fed to you by your schools. BUT! You are allowed to underline the actions in a fiction passage. This will mean that

approximately 2% of the fiction passage should be underlined, not 98!
Gives a stern look

You also don't need to underline it. You can just make a note in your
head. But, it can be useful to know the location to which you should
return when you hit the questions pertaining to the actions.

Practice

When you're reading fiction passages, look for any actual actions that
happen. Underline them or don't. Just be sure to remember them.
You should probably also include them in your SRS. If there is ONE
action in the entire passage, and you don't mention it in your SUM-
MARY...then you may need to revisit the dictionary on the definition
of the word "summary"!

When you get to the questions, keep that action (and your SRS) in
mind!

Science and Social Science passages

For these passages, you should focus on OPINIONS.

Most scientific passages will have a lot of facts. That means, just like
actions in a fiction passage, any opinions should really stand out. If
there are any expressed, you'll probably see 1-3 questions pertaining
to that one opinion. So, again here, highlight it or don't, but definitely
pay attention to it.

Furthermore, if the opinions expressed are really intense, you will
definitely see 2 or more related questions. Identifying the intensity of
an opinion takes practice, so think about intensity with every scientific
passage you read.

If you're not sure how to tell, you need to get outside help. Come
work with us at VohraMethod.com, or ask any highly literary parents,
aunts/uncles, etc. you have. Obviously, don't ask your teachers.

Historical and Dual Passages

Historical and dual passages are opposite the science ones; they will almost completely contain opinions. For the dual passages, you should obviously focus on where the two people agree and disagree (aka, find their theses). That's the whole point of those passages, and at least half of the questions will reference those points of disagreement and agreement either directly or indirectly.

The more important aspect of the historical passages is that they are all written in a more complex way because they were written hundreds of years ago (often by pompous and exceedingly verbose dudes). So, **you need to know your grammar very well**.

Lucky for you, there's a whole grammar section on the SAT anyways! So, you'll end up learning the grammar you'll need in my Three-Week Grammar Crash Course!

All you really need to know is that it's hard to do well on the Historical passages unless you have a firm grasp of core grammar components: **prepositional phrases, modifying clauses, infinitives, subjects and direct objects, and the very basic notion of what a modifier is.**

Tactic 3: Disprove; Don't Prove

Due to your upbringing in a school environment, you're probably used to writing "essays". This is basically where you pretend to read a miserable book that you hate, then you pick out quotes from that book (basically at random) and you use those quotes to "prove" some kind of terrible thesis. This is all no offense to you, obviously. The offense is all to your school. But, sadly, this process has taught you three things:

1. How to write something that is almost certainly NOT a thesis.
2. How to use pretty much ANY evidence to prove ANY claim.
3. How to bullshit.

Now, the value of #3 is arguable, but the big problem we have for the SAT is #2. You are so used to using any nonsensical evidence to prove any ridiculous claim that you are going to get things wrong on the test IF you use the same methods.

Here's how this usually plays out:

Mental Gymnastics:

Well, in the passage, Bob is wearing a yellow tie. Yellow is the color of springtime and hope. The springtime is when the world comes alive again. New trees, baby animals, pretty flowers. But it's winter in this story right now. So, either Bob is having a baby (new birth/springtime), or Bob is confused and has conflicting emotions.

Let's all stop and take a moment to laugh at this nonsense.

HAAHHAHhahahaahahaha

Okay great. But here's the deal. You have DEFinitely done this in your own brain before. **Every single one of my students** has done it live in front of me! You've probably done it so many times that it doesn't even seem weird anymore.

Schools have gone so heavy on symbolism and "deeper meaning" that they've contorted "reading" into a task where you basically just make stuff up that the author maybe/probably/definitely never intended. Schools have turned reading into an interpretation act, instead of an opportunity to access the sharp mind of another individual.

And, as always, you are the one who suffers. First, because no one enjoys an interpretation act where one person pretends he/she knows THE answer. And second, because now you're failing the SAT.

On the SAT, things are a lot more straightforward. They sort of have to be, and you should understand why.

If it ever came out that the College Board (the company making the test) were creating subjective questions, questions that could arguably be either A or B, or maybe even C, depending on how you "interpret" the passage...well, you can be sure that a lot of parents would draw up a class action lawsuit quick, fast, and in a big hurry.

They simply cannot create ambiguous questions. There's always a clear reason why the answer is B, not A.

So, why do you have to disprove, not prove?

Because you're very used to proving nonsense using nonsense. But, you're not very used to DISproving at all. Most students don't do a lot of Proof by Contradiction, and your school is less interested in your disproving false claims about a passage than in proving whatever new fluffy idea **might** be true about whatever boring book.

This is great! It means you have a tool you can use. And, it turns out, almost every one of my students in many years of tutoring has been terrible at proving, but pretty great at disproving!

Key Skill: Disprove Using ONE Word

This is just an extension of Disprove Don't Prove, and it's intended to help focus your efforts. If even one, tiny fraction of an answer choice is wrong, then that entire answer choice is super wrong, so don't pick it.

Here's an example answer choice:

(A) says "the narrator's attitude shifts from fear about the expedition to excitement about it".

So, we ask ourselves, is the narrator showing "fear"? If not, then A is wrong.

If the narrator is showing fear, then is that fear "about the expedition" or about something else? If it's about something else, then A is wrong.

If the fear is about the expedition, then we see if he's showing "excitement".

If he is showing excitement, then we see if the excitement is about "the expedition".

And, if all those things are true, then we need to ask if the narrator shifts "from" the fear "to" the excitement. In other words, is the narrator afraid at the beginning of the passage, and excited at the end? If the order is reversed, then A is wrong.

I know that seems like a lot of steps, but you'll pick it up quickly. For my students, just knowing that there are clear steps and progressive questions you can ask yourself seems to assuage a lot of the anxiety around the test questions and answers.

Key Skill: Ask Yourself, "What would _______ look like?"

Sometimes you're stuck between two answers. Actually, that probably happens a lot! When you get to that place, this skill can be really helpful.

Also, for some mystical reason, almost every single student I've worked with is just magically good at this skill with little to no practice. It's a simple idea, so be sure to keep it simple!

You just ask yourself, "What would it look like if A were true?"

Here's an example answer choice:

The sentence in lines 10-13 mainly serves to…

(B) demonstrate that the narrator thinks in a methodical and scientific manner.

Ask yourself, "If the passage were really trying to show that Dudeface McGee 'thinks in a methodical and scientific manner', what would that look like?"

Well, you'd probably see him approaching a problem and thinking it through. He would probably use a lot of If Then statements, or maybe create a hypothesis and then a test for that hypothesis.

You guys all KNOW what science looks like, at least at a basic level. Hypothesis, test, controls, variables, results, conclusion.

You also KNOW what a method looks like.

Remember, **this book is about unlocking your inherent superpowers.** So, work with what you know.

Side note: the more you know, the better your whole life will generally be. Knowledge is gained by books.

Read more books! But, specifically not any of the books your school recommends. Some of them might not be terrible, but they are proba-bly all very boring. If you want some book recommendations, send me an email. I can give you a ton of ideas completely free.

We're going to practice Disprove Don't Prove very soon. Generally, you should practice it in every practice test and passage you read.

~~Tactic~~ Rule 4: DO NOT answer the question + evidence paired questions at the same time

I repeat: Do not, under any circumstances, look at a question and its paired evidence question and answer them simultaneously!! DO NOT do it!

Why?

1. The SAT is trying to trick you.
2. The paired questions are the single most powerful tool the SAT has for tricking you.
3. Students almost always get either both right or BOTH WRONG. That's two questions gone. You can't afford that.
4. **Most importantly:** The SAT pairs up the evidence answer choices with the original question answer choices.

I'll elaborate. Let's say the initial question's correct answer is B, and the evidence (in the next question) is D. Guess what? The pair A and C is going to make **a lot** of sense. The evidence in C is going to perfectly support answer A for the initial question. AND! The evidence in B is going to seem quite supportive of answer C for the initial question.

So, if you look at those two questions together, and you're looking for a pair of answers that seem to reinforce each other, you're going to find them. You're going to find 2+ sets of them.

That won't help you narrow down your answers, and it will almost certainly cause you to lose points. So, stop doing it now and forever.

Very Strict Rule: When you see an evidence question coming (and you always know, because there are a bunch of line numbers, parentheses, and quotes in the answer choices), **you must physically cover up the evidence question** until you have finished answering the initial question AND picking out your own preferred evidence to support your answer.

It looks like this:

Question 19 is a regular question. Question 20 is evidence for Question 19.

1. Physically cover up Question 20 so that you cannot see it at all. No peeking! Your SAT score is at stake.
2. Pick your answer for Question 19.
3. Find evidence in the passage that supports your answer for Question 19. Still no peeking at Question 20!
4. Finally, uncover Question 20 and see if your evidence is one of the options. If not, look for something very close to the evidence you picked. If there is nothing remotely close to your chosen evidence, then re-cover Question 20 and think about your answer for Question 19 again.

Ignore this rule at your own peril!

Also, if you do ignore this rule, and you get BOTH questions wrong in a Question + Evidence pair...then allow me to offer my heartfelt laughter. Remember to laugh at yourself a good bit for ignoring this rule and suffering the consequences. Then, stop ignoring this rule and start dominating the SAT.

Teaching Test

Now we need to put those rules and tactics into practice! If I show you one time how to kick a soccer ball, you're not going to instantly become a professional player. You have to practice a lot. So, let's go practice as much as we possibly can.

However! This isn't a regular "practice" test or a diagnostic. The following is a Teaching Test. You should follow along and complete each piece as it comes up. I'll explain every tiny nuance I can in the texts and the questions, and I'll help you analyze why you got a question right or wrong.

For this Teaching Test, I am using College Board's Test 4. **Go to this webpage so you can download the PDF version of the test:** www.VohraMethod.com/Reading-Crash-Course

You'll need the PDF version so you can have the line numbers referenced in the questions, but I'll include the plain text passages in this book for easy reading.

Test 4 is no longer on College Board's website, so I've included it on our website for free.

Fiction Passage

This passage is adapted from MacDonald Harris, *The Balloonist*. ©2011 by The Estate of Donald Heiney. During the summer of 1897, the narrator of this story, a fictional Swedish scientist, has set out for the North Pole in a hydrogen-powered balloon.

My emotions are complicated and not readily verifiable. I feel a vast yearning that is simultaneously a pleasure and a pain. I am certain of the consummation of this yearning, but I don't know yet what form it will take, since I do not understand quite what it is that the yearning desires. For the first time there is borne in upon me the full truth of what I myself said to the doctor only an hour ago: that my motives in this undertaking are not entirely clear. For years, for a lifetime, the machinery of my destiny has worked in secret to prepare for this moment; its clockwork has moved exactly toward this time and place and no other. Rising slowly from the earth that bore me and gave me sustenance, I am carried helplessly toward an uninhabited and hostile, or at best indifferent, part of the earth, littered with the bones of explorers and the wrecks of ships, frozen supply caches, messages scrawled with chilled fingers and hidden in cairns that no eye will ever see. Nobody has succeeded in this thing, and many have died. Yet in freely willing this enterprise, in choosing this moment and no other when the south wind will carry me exactly northward at a velocity of eight knots, I have converted the machinery of my fate into the servant of my will. All this I understand, as I understand each detail of the technique by which this is carried out. What I don't understand is why I am so intent on going to this particular place. Who wants the North Pole! What good is it! Can you eat it? Will it carry you from Gothenburg to Malmö like a railway? The Danish ministers have declared from their pulpits that participation in polar expeditions is beneficial to the soul's eternal well-being, or so I read in a newspaper. It isn't clear how this doctrine is to be interpreted, except that the Pole is something difficult or impossible to attain which must nevertheless be sought for, because man is condemned to seek out and know everything whether or not the knowledge gives him pleasure. In short, it is the same unthinking lust for knowledge that drove our First Parents out of the garden.

And suppose you were to find it in spite of all, this wonderful place that everybody is so anxious to stand on! *What* would you find? Exactly nothing. A point precisely identical to all the others in a completely featureless wasteland stretching around it for hundreds of miles. It is an abstraction, a mathematical fiction. No one but a Swedish madman could take the slightest interest in it. Here I am. The wind is still from the south, bearing us steadily northward at the speed of a trotting dog. Behind us, perhaps forever, lie the Cities of Men with their teacups and their brass bedsteads. I am going forth of my own volition to join the ghosts of Bering and poor Franklin, of frozen DeLong and his men. What I am on the brink of knowing, I now see, is not an ephemeral mathematical spot but myself. The doctor was right, even though I dislike him. Fundamentally I am a dangerous madman, and what I do is both a challenge to my egotism and a surrender to it.

Alright! Do your Simple **Ridiculous** Summary. Here's a reminder of the rules:

1. You must use the phrase "be like".
2. You must use no more than two sentences.
3. Your summary must be comprehensible to a 5-year-old.
4. Your summary must NOT include any of the words from the passage.

For your SRS, you should have gotten something like this:

This dude is trying to go to the North Pole, but he be like, "Why do I even want to go there? Weird."

Every 5 year old now understands that passage. The only words I used from the passage were "North Pole". I obviously included "be like". And, I kept it short!

If your SRS is lacking or failing to meet any of the rules above, come meet with me. It is often VERY hard for students to write something as heinous as "be like". I have watched students become physically uncomfortable when I encouraged them to just try it in a tutoring session.

I get it. I was a rule-follower in high school. I would never have done something that would cause my English teacher to so deeply disapprove of me. In the face of that much disapproval, I might have just died. BUT! Your English teacher has already failed you, so stop trying to please him/her. Quit it now. Do something better. Use English bad. Proceed.

Focus: Next, you need to focus on any actions that actually happen in this passage (because it's a fiction passage!). See if you can find any actions in this passage. Write them down. (Answers will generally come right after any large horizontal lines, so no peeking!)

Having trouble? It turns out, there is only ONE action! "The wind is still from the south, bearing us steadily northward at the speed of a trotting dog."

So, the only action here is that the wind blew. Seriously, that's it.

Sure, the Danish ministers said some stuff **in the past** that gets referenced here. But we're looking for anything that happens **during** this passage's events. And here, it's just the wind blowing…

When I said very few actions, I really meant it!

I will note that this one action doesn't help you much. There will be one question pertaining to that sentence, but it's a Vocab question, not comprehension. Still, it's useful to practice your focus, as it will help you in other passages.

Two notes before getting into the questions:

First: The best way to get a perfect score in the reading section is to know how to disprove every wrong answer choice just as confidently as you feel you can select the correct answer choice. So, I will walk you through almost every answer choice for the first couple of passages.

It'll be a lot of reading at first, but you'll need less and less direction and guidance as we go along. So, don't worry; I won't pontificate forever (this is still a crash course, after all!).

Second: For every question, you MUST go into the passage and pick out the supporting evidence. Once you find your evidence, write down the few words you used, or the line numbers of longer quotes, just like the SAT does. If you don't do this, you might as well just set your time on fire.

You need to get into the strong habit of looking for real, clear evidence in the passage to **support or disprove every single answer choice.** Really put your Disproving Skills to the test on the following passages. Now is the time to learn, not the time to complete-everything-really-fast-and-be-finished-but-you-learned-nothing. Don't be dumb.

Question 1

Over the course of the passage, the narrator's attitude shifts from

(A) fear about the expedition to excitement about it.

(B) doubt about his abilities to confidence in them.

(C) uncertainty of his motives to recognition of them.

(D) disdain for the North Pole to appreciation of it.

Pick your answer, **find your supporting evidence**, then check your answer on the following pages.

Read over all the wrong answers, too, so you can practice disproving! When you're stuck on the real test, I promise you that your ability to disprove a wrong answer will matter more than your ability to prove the correct answer.

What you should learn from A:

This answer choice is a frequent wrong guess, and it usually comes from a predictable place. You saw that a lot of people died in these expeditions. Maybe you saw the word "helplessly" (line 15) or the word "dangerous" (line 59). But, none of those things helps support answer choice A.

Important Admonishment: DO NOT cherry pick single words out of the passage, ignoring their context, and then blindly pick an answer!

So, **ask yourself, "What would a passage look like if it were trying to show that the narrator is afraid?"** Think about it for a minute before reading on.

Well, the passage might say something like "I am afraid" (lol). Or, maybe you would see phrases like, "it sends shivers down my spine", "I shake at the thought of it", "I find myself constantly checking over my shoulder". These are all the standard tropes of the horror genre. Even if you've never seen a horror film, you've probably accidentally seen a horror film trailer.

General Rule: Use what you know. You KNOW what fear looks like. Shaking, goosebumps, feeling frozen, anxious, checking behind you, wanting to have the lights on, closing all the window blinds, heart racing, etc.

Do we see any of that in this passage? No.

Just because everyone died on the journey, doesn't mean that this narrator is afraid of the trip. A lot of people have died skydiving. Some people aren't afraid of skydiving. YOU might be afraid of skydiving. And you might be afraid of a trip on which everyone before you died. But…

Important Admonishment: You can't project your own emotions into the characters in the story! (obviously)

What you should learn from B:

Again here, the SAT is counting on your taking a bunch of pieces of evidence out of context and misinterpreting them.

Lines 4-5 contain the words "I don't know yet". Lines 9-10 contain the words "not entirely clear". That could support doubt, right?

Later, we see "freely willing this enterprise" in line 21 and "all this I understand" in line 25. Don't those sort of support "confidence"?

Important Admonishment: Disprove; don't Prove!! This is such a good example of why. Sure, you can "prove" the word doubt, and you can "prove" the word confidence. But, the answer choice doesn't say, "doubt confidence". The answer choice says, "doubt **about his abilities** to confidence **in them**". In the passage, the narrator's uncertainty pertains to his "motives" not his "abilities". (Also, uncertainty is not the same as doubt. Do your Vocab Synapse!)

So, disprove; don't prove. Also, try asking yourself, **"What would this passage look like if it were showing 'doubt about his abilities'?"**

Diving Deeper into C:

Correct! **This answer choice lines up perfectly with our SRS** of a Swedish dude who's like, "idk why I want to go to the North Pole, but I guess I'm going anyways! Maybe I'm crazy!" Remember to keep your SRS close at hand. You'll see how many questions it can help you with now that we're getting started!

That said…**I'm guessing you weren't 100% sure about the evidence for "recognition of them".** Go ahead and take a minute to reread the passage and look for the evidence for the "recognition of his motives" before moving on.

If you picked D:

D is an uncommon wrong answer. If you picked it, it's possible that you just aren't 100% clear on what "disdain" means. **If you haven't already, start your Vocab Synapse training.**

Also, note that if you're picking several uncommon or weird wrong answers, you should get outside help. I would love to help you overcome every obstacle and achieve your greatest success. Otherwise, look for someone who reads constantly and knows how to cut the nonsense.

Question 2

Which choice provides the best evidence for the answer to the previous question?

Before I show you the answers…you'll notice I didn't even show you this question when you were doing Question 1. **Remember never to look at these together or attempt to answer them together!**

But, when you do get to the evidence question, you need to pay very close attention to **what you are supposed to be proving.** You might be surprised by the number of students who get the initial question correct, the evidence question wrong, and then they tell me, "Oh my gosh, I didn't even think about the first question when picking this evidence!"

You guys like to fixate on one word in the correct answer choice for the initial question. Or you might focus on a small part of the question itself and ignore the answer choice you picked. Both of those are obviously bad.

Here's what you should do: underline or circle both the initial question and the answer you picked, reread it all together, then go looking for evidence for that.

Initial Question and Answer: Over the course of the passage, the narrator's attitude shifts from...uncertainty of his motives to recognition of them.

So, ideally we're looking for evidence that proves BOTH the "uncertainty of his motives" and the later "recognition". Based on the evidence you already found when you were doing Question 1...you should have a good idea of where to look.

Which choice provides the best evidence for the answer to the previous question?

    (A) Lines 10-12 ("For ... moment")
    (B) Lines 21-25 ("Yet ... will")
    (C) Lines 42-44 ("And ... stand on")
    (D) Lines 56-57 ("What ... myself")

If you picked A:

No. Make sure you're not distracted. A doesn't have either uncertainty OR recognition of his motives in it.

If you are distracted, put this book down and come back later. **You cannot possibly expect to do a crash course with anything less than 1000% focus.**

If you did have some logic for picking A, now is a good time to talk to a professional tutor. You need to know where your lines of reasoning are failing you so that you can correct your thinking and accel. I've worked with hundreds of kids over the years who had weird ideas and justifications for picking whichever answer. Sometimes, the logic makes sense, and we need to look for extra evidence to clearly disprove your reasoning. Sometimes, you're just engaging in Mental Gymnastics and you need to take a moment to laugh at yourself for that style of thinking.

It's hard to know for sure if you don't have someone to consult with. If you want to set up a 30-minute meeting, you can find me at www.VohraMethod.com.

Making an example out of B:

Many of the students who pick this answer were thinking along these lines: "This quote is showing that the narrator is taking control of his destiny. Taking control requires confidence. Confidence is the opposite of uncertainty (sort of). We're looking for a change from uncertainty to something else, so…it's B!"

Important Admonishment: Don't do Mental Gymnastics!

You can be confident and still uncertain if there are just things you don't know. You can be confident and still not "recognize your motives". And, most importantly, **the SAT is always more straightforward than you think it's being.** Sure, they're trying to trick you. But, you'll quickly discover that the real evidence is a one-step thought process. It's generally pretty clear, not a string of 15 mental backflips.

The part of the passage that most clearly shows the "uncertainty of his motives" part is lines 9-10: "my motives in this undertaking are not entirely clear". That is VERY direct, nearly word for word. THAT is what you should generally be looking for.

If you picked C:

C is another uncommon answer.

If you are distracted, put this book down and come back later. **You cannot possibly expect to do a crash course with anything less than 1000% focus.**

If you did have some logic for picking C, look for a professional tutor to help you!

If you picked D:

Correct! Now, this one is still hard. So, just in case you picked D on accident…

"What I am on the brink of knowing, I now see, is not an ephemeral mathematical spot but myself."

Everything you need is contained within the three tiny words "brink of knowing".

When you are "on the brink" it means you're on the edge of something…and there's some other big thing coming next. If you're on the brink of a cliff, then what's behind you is land, and what's coming next is…a really big fall. But, if you're on the "brink of knowing", then what's behind you is the NOT knowing, and what's coming next is knowing. **Not knowing = uncertainty. Knowing = recognition.**

This is not mental gymnastics. This is just simple and true.

Now, if you think about it a bit, you can understand the concept of "being on the brink". And, if you think a little more, you can apply that general concept to all sorts of situations. You could think about what it might mean to be "on the brink of happiness" or "on the brink of success" or "on the brink of failure".

But! It's still not a very common thing. So, when you first read that sentence, you probably didn't immediately think of it as a cliff with **not knowing** behind you and **knowing** in front of you.

That's fair. But, you need to change that. **The only solution to issues like this is to read…a lot.** The SAT knows this. That's why they include passages with hard phrases, and questions that use specific hard phrases as evidence. They are genuinely trying to test your core reading skill and ability.

Important Note: In three weeks, you have enough time to read something.

> » Pick up a few books from the SAT book list (Appendix C) and just **read one chapter at random from each book**. If you have time, read two chapters.
> » You don't need to know the story.
> » You DO need to **make flashcards for ALL vocabulary you didn't know.**
> » You DO need to **look up any phrases you don't understand**, or get someone to explain it to you, simply and clearly (not a big pile of fluffy metaphor and nonsense).

Doing this will pay off more than you can imagine.

Question 3

As used in lines 1-2, "not readily verifiable" most nearly means

    (A) unable to be authenticated.
    (B) likely to be contradicted.
    (C) without empirical support.
    (D) not completely understood.

This question really teaches you how to laugh at answer choices, even when they're all smart-sounding and dense.

Give it a shot, find your evidence or jot down your logical reasoning, and then review.

Let's laugh at A:

The sentence with A is: My emotions are complicated and unable to be authenticated.

To the trained eye, choice A is hilarious.

Key Tip: When you look at questions and answers like this, with so many big words that you may or may not know, ask yourself, "What sorts of things are ________________?"

In this case, what sorts of things get authenticated?

This is something that you KNOW the answer to because you've lived life on the planet earth for more than 5 years.

Passwords get authenticated. ID cards and passports get authenticated. Your identity must be authenticated every time you log in to your email, various personal accounts, bank accounts, etc. Even if you don't have a bank account, you know that banks don't just **believe** anyone who walks into a bank claiming to be Elon Musk…

Art is proven to be either authentic or a fake. Someone's personality might be referred to as "authentic" (aka real) or fake. You **know** what a fake and superficial person looks like.

Authentic means it's the REAL thing. Authentic Louis Vuitton bags vs fake knock offs.

The point is, start from what you know. What does it mean for emotions to be "unable to be authenticated"? Well, no one can even really read such nonsense… So, make it simple.

You know what sorts of things are usually "authenticated". Now ask yourself, are emotions usually "authenticated"? Do we think to ourselves, "I'm not sure if I'm actually feeling this emotion or not. Let me verify that I am feeling this emotion using some kind of test."

No. We do not.

Furthermore, the answer choice says UNABLE to be authenticated!

Which means you tried to figure out if you're actually feeling the emotion that you're feeling, you weren't sure, you did your tests, and the tests failed to tell you if you are or are not feeling that emotion! So... you still don't know!

Now, I know that some emotions may feel a bit complex...but that is just nonsense.

Key Skill: Recognize complete nonsense...and laugh at it! (There will be a lot of nonsense on the SAT.)

If you picked C:

Nope!

The sentence with C is: My emotions are complicated and without empirical support.

Again here, hopefully you can start to see the hilarity of some of these answers. Sure, you picked it this time, but the goal is to grow from here, not to be perfect right away. If you were already perfect, that would only mean that you had already put in the necessary work prior to now.

So, first, if you didn't know the meaning of "empirical", go look it up right now and create a flashcard for yourself. This is a word you need to know.

Next, do we usually require "empirical support" for our emotions? Do you often think to yourself, "Self, I believe we are feeling confidence right now, but we should probably create a scientific experiment to test and observe this emotion so that we can verify that it is, in fact, 'confidence' that we are feeling." And then your Self says back to you, "Cheerio ol' chap! Science is Phun!" Or something...

Okay, point is, that's not what you or anyone has ever done. We don't need verifiable support for our emotions because we human beings are the only ones who can verify our own emotions, anyways.

Have a good laugh and keep reading!

Answer D and the SRS:

For this, you can go back to your Simple, Ridiculous Summary again. The SRS for this passage is: Some dude be like, "I'm going to the North Pole and I don't know why!"

A huge part of that is the "I don't know why" bit. When an answer choice lines up THAT nicely with your SRS, you can start to really consider picking it.

Question 4

The sentence in lines 10-13 ("For years . . . other") mainly serves to

- **(A)** expose a side of the narrator that he prefers to keep hidden.
- **(B)** demonstrate that the narrator thinks in a methodical and scientific manner.
- **(C)** show that the narrator feels himself to be influenced by powerful and independent forces.
- **(D)** emphasize the length of time during which the narrator has prepared for his expedition.

Pick your answer and write down a quick analysis/explanation before continuing! (By the way, I recommend you write these down because then you can definitively see what you were thinking. If you don't... well, I've had a lot of students who delude themselves into thinking that they were "pretty close" when in reality they just had a jumble of nonsense thoughts in their head that happen to contain 3 of the same words as the sensible explanation. Don't fall victim to delusions. Just write down your explanations and practice getting your ideas onto paper!)

Okay, so the answer here is C. If you picked C, cool.

Most of my students don't pick C because they don't really get what this bit is saying. They also always tell me that they don't really like any of the other answer choices and they just picked whichever one because they weren't sure. But, a surprising number of students tell me that the one they know it FOR SURE is not, is C.

At this point, we have a good laugh at them =) But, it brings up an important point.

Important Admonishment: Don't just discount something because you don't "get it"! Instead, if you don't understand one answer choice, skip it and work on disproving the other three.

If you can definitively disprove the other three, then that confusing answer choice is probably right… If you find a different answer choice that you can't disprove, then that one is probably the answer. Simple as that.

So, A talks about a side of the narrator that he prefers to keep hidden. Ask yourself, "Is this narrator a super secretive or shameful guy?" Also, "What would the passage look like if it were showing a guy who wants to hide part of himself?"

I'd be willing to bet that you have seen a mystery movie or read a book at some point in your life. You know what mysterious, secretive people look like. It's not this guy.

B talks about a scientific and methodical manner. What would that look like? The narrator would probably be discussing a particular problem with wind patterns or weight ratios and how to solve that problem using various resources and clear steps. Do we see that? Nope.

Now, D is the common wrong answer. You all like to read the words "for years, for a lifetime" and then immediately pick D. To which I say…"hahaaahhahahaahahah Ha." Quit it. Stop doin' that. Laugh at yourself, and then cease and desist!

If the passage were really trying to show that, you'd see stuff like, "Five years ago, I started putting together my crew. Four years ago, I was discussing plans for supplies and weight capacities. It took 3 years to find the right balloon for the journey. I spent years studying the paths other explorers took…" etc. You would see a clear discussion of all the work that went in and all the time it took.

D doesn't just say "emphasize the length of time". D says, "emphasize the length of time **during which the narrator has prepared for his expedition**".

But **now we need to understand what C is talking about.** Cool, we disproved the others, but let's also definitively prove C. C says the narrator is influenced by powerful and independent forces. The quote from the passage is:

For years, for a lifetime, the machinery of my destiny has worked in secret to prepare for this moment; its clockwork has moved exactly toward this time and place and no other.

Here's where a bit of grammar comes in. What is the main verb in the first clause? (If you don't know the first thing about grammar, I highly recommend enrolling in the Accelerated Grammar Course I created. You can finish it in 12 hours or less, if you work hard. So, you could finish it in one week. Grammar is critical for advanced reading, as you'll see more clearly in just a couple of passages. Alternatively, check out my Grammar Crash Course book.)

The main verb in the first clause is "has worked". And what is the subject of that verb?

"the machinery of my destiny"

So, this sentence isn't even really about the narrator at all. This sentence is about the machinery of the narrator's destiny. What does that mean?

It's just talking about destiny or fate. The concept of destiny is being personified. I like to imagine Mr. Destiny looking down on our narrator, pulling levers on his Destiny Machine, making stuff happen in the narrator's life, and probably chuckling. No wonder the narrator has no idea why he wants to go to the North Pole! It's Mr. Destiny pulling his strings like a puppet. The narrator is just sort of blindly following the path that Mr. Destiny lays out (at least until line 24).

So, what are these "powerful and independent forces" in C? They are Destiny and Fate.

I get it if you didn't see all that the first or even fourth time you read this passage. That's what this practice is for. You'll pick it up and start seeing personification more readily, ridiculous answers more clearly, etc. Fear not!

Question 5

The narrator indicates that many previous explorers seeking the North Pole have

- **(A)** perished in the attempt.
- **(B)** made surprising discoveries.
- **(C)** failed to determine its exact location.
- **(D)** had different motivations than h is own.

Pick your answer and find your evidence! There is clear, textual evidence for this one, for sure.

The answer here is A. We'll discuss evidence in a bit.

If you picked any other answer, figure out how you could disprove that answer now.

For example, nowhere in the passage does it mention the motivations of any of the other explorers who attempted this journey. Now, the general rule is that **the absence of evidence does NOT equal evidence of absence**. In other words, just because something isn't directly stated, doesn't mean it isn't true.

However, if the passage were going to indicate that other explorers had different motivations than the narrator's, they would definitely have to tell you at least ONE other motivation!

Also…the narrator doesn't even know his OWN motivations for going (that's the whole SRS again). So, D is a bit silly.

Do that for B or C, if you picked either of those. There is very good evidence against B that just so happens to be the same as the evidence supporting A.

Then continue with your evidence picked out to the next question!

Question 6

Speaking of evidence supporting A...

Which choice provides the best evidence for the answer to the previous question?

- **(A)** Lines 20-21 ("Nobody ... died")
- **(B)** Lines 25-27 ("All ... out")
- **(C)** Lines 31-34 ("The ... newspaper")
- **(D)** Lines 51-53 ("Behind ... bedsteads")

Make sure you have the prior question + answer choice written out so you know what you're proving!

Okay! This one probably went pretty quickly. The answer is A. Hopefully it was pretty obvious, just from the word "died" in there…(lol)

Question 7

Which choice best describes the narrator's view of his expedition to
the North Pole?

    (A) Immoral but inevitable
    (B) Absurd but necessary
    (C) Socially beneficial but misunderstood
    (D) Scientifically important but hazardous

Pick your answer and get some evidence up in here!

This type of question is the best opportunity to practice Disprove; don't Prove. It's all actually just individual words which you can individually disprove!

Now, most students see the word "misunderstood" and they start to **really** like C. I encourage this, because it means that you're applying your SRS, which was all about confusion and stuff.

BUT! You then have to try to disprove "socially beneficial" and see if it holds up. Look for direct evidence against "socially beneficial". There is a clear quote.

The narrator starts his discussion of the Pole's uselessness in line 28 with "Who wants the North Pole! What good is it!" and then really gets to the point in line 44 with "What would you find? Exactly nothing."

So, if you're finding nothing, then it's not socially beneficial. But wait Chelsey! What about lines 31-34 which literally contain the word beneficial in them!?!

Good point dear student. Let's revisit the question at hand:

Which choice best describes **the narrator's view** of his expedition to the North Pole? Lines 31-34 are not the narrator's view. They showcase the viewpoint of "the Danish ministers".

Remember how I said that reading the questions carefully is important and stuff? Yep…

Okay! We disproved "socially beneficial". We can also use the same evidence to disprove "scientifically important", even though "hazardous" would certainly be true. If you're finding "nothing", then you're not really contributing to science.

Now, most students like "inevitable" because of the whole Destiny and Fate thing from before. But, is this trip immoral?

No. A trip can't really be immoral. If humanity went on a trip to a distant planet and accidentally killed the alien life forms living there… the **trip** still wouldn't be immoral. Maybe the killing was immoral, but the trip was just movement.

Which leaves us with B, at which point everyone says, "How is it necessary?!? Isn't it useless?" It turns out, something can be both of those things. More importantly, go find the evidence supporting "necessary"! It is only 6 words, stuck in the middle of a sentence somewhere in the passage, and it will be hard to find. Read the passage slowly, twice. Consider this your first real challenge!

The evidence is found in lines 35-37: "…the Pole is something difficult or impossible to attain **which must nevertheless be sought for.**"

If you couldn't find it, why do you think that is? Because you're not used to words like "nevertheless" and "sought" so your brain tends to just tune those words out, skim over them, breeze right on by…

Again, go read as many books as you can. Get used to these more complicated phrasings. Trust me, complex English doesn't magically disappear when you become an adult.

Anyways, if a thing MUST be sought for, then it is necessary. The narrator says that, of all that the Danish ministers are saying, this is the only part that he is clear on.

This is an awesome example of what really good evidence looks like. Five words tucked inside a much longer sentence, hidden in a dense paragraph. It may sound impossible, but you'll get there (and quickly).

Question 8

The question the narrator asks in lines 30-31 ("Will it . . . railway")
most nearly implies that

> **(A)** balloons will never replace other modes of transportation.
> **(B)** the North Pole is farther away than the cities usually reached
> by train.
> **(C)** people often travel from one city to another without consider-
> ing the implications.
> **(D)** reaching the North Pole has no foreseeable benefit to humanity.

Here's the full question in line 30:

Will it carry you from Gothenburg to Malmö like a railway?

Select your answer and write down your reasoning.

This question is a GREAT example of taking things out of context.
The SAT loves this trick, so get used to it and don't fall for it!

Now, if you look at only the question, you might think the answer is A
(because railways are also transportation) or B (because B mentions a
train). That's not how SAT answers work; hopefully you know this by
now!

You need to be reading all the surrounding text, the entire question,
and the entire answer choice (not just one word in it).

With a little reflection, you can see that A and B are hilariously
wrong. This author isn't concerned with whether or not balloons will
become popular as a mode of transportation (and also, obviously they
will not! Lol). Also, **of course** the North Pole is farther away than
most of the **super close by** cities to which people often travel. This is
the late 1800s. The world was far less global and connected. The plane
hadn't yet been invented. (That happens in 1903 by the way, but you
don't need to know facts like that. You could reasonably assume that,
if this dude is taking a balloon of all things…then maybe there are no
planes yet. But still, it's a cool milestone in history to know about.)

Okay so, A is silly, and B is obtuse.

C is BOTH silly and obtuse! What on earth possible "implications"
could there be of going to visit your grandma in the next city over?
This gets back to that one answer choice that suggested the trip to the
North Pole might be "immoral". It's just a pile of nonsense.

So, the answer is D. If you got this one wrong, take a second to try to
find the evidence that clearly supports D.

Obviously lines 30-31 have some of it. But, again here we're focusing
on line 44: "What would you find? Exactly nothing." The narrator
clearly thinks that the expedition won't have any benefit at all. That's
why it's so weird that he wants to go.

Question 9

As used in line 49, "take the slightest interest in" most nearly means

> **(A)** accept responsibility for.
> **(B)** possess little regard for.
> **(C)** pay no attention to.
> **(D)** have curiosity about.

Pick your answer and write down your thoughts/reasoning.

There's no big trick here, and nothing bizarre of note. The answer is D.

You can use your SRS to get this one. The SRS says that this passage is about a kinda crazy dude who wants to go to the North Pole but he doesn't know why. He is curious, though!

Question 10

As used in line 50, "bearing" most nearly means

    (A) carrying.
    (B) affecting.
    (C) yielding.
    (D) enduring.

Answer and explanation!

The answer is A.

Occasionally, I'll have a student get this one wrong. The reason is usually just a lack of familiarity with the word "bearing". Bearing is a common word used in weather to talk about wind and weather movements. You might hear, "The wind is bearing down on us from the North" or something like that.

So, watch the weather channel more? Lol.

But actually, make sure you're doing your Vocab Synapse!

Social Science Passage

This passage is adapted from Alan Ehrenhalt, *The Great Inversion and the Future of the American City*. ©2013 by Vintage. Ehrenhalt is an urbanologist—a scholar of cities and their development. Demographic inversion is a phenomenon that describes the rearrangement of living patterns throughout a metropolitan area.

We are not witnessing the abandonment of the suburbs, or a movement of millions of people back to the city all at once. The 2010 census certainly did not turn up evidence of a middle-class stampede to the nation's cities. The news was mixed: Some of the larger cities on the East Coast tended to gain population, albeit in small increments. Those in the Midwest, including Chicago, tended to lose substantial numbers. The cities that showed gains in overall population during the entire decade tended to be in the South and Southwest. But when it comes to measuring demographic inversion, raw census numbers are an ineffective blunt instrument. A closer look at the results shows that the most powerful demographic events of the past decade were the movement of African Americans out of central cities (180,000 of them in Chicago alone) and the settlement of immigrant groups in suburbs, often ones many miles distant from downtown. Central-city areas that gained affluent residents in the first part of the decade maintained that population in the recession years from 2007 to 2009. They also, according to a 2011 study by Brookings, suffered considerably less from increased unemployment than the suburbs did. Not many young professionals moved to new downtown condos in the recession years because few such residences were being built. But there is no reason to believe that the demographic trends prevailing prior to the construction bust will not resume once that bust is over. It is important to remember that demographic inversion is not a proxy for population growth; it can occur in cities that are growing, those whose numbers are flat, and even in those undergoing a modest decline in size.

America's major cities face enormous fiscal problems, many of them the result of public pension obligations they incurred in the more prosperous years of the past two decades. Some, Chicago prominent among them, simply are not producing enough revenue to support the level of public services to which most of the citizens have grown to feel entitled. How the cities are going to solve this problem, I do not know. What I do know is that if fiscal crisis were going to drive affluent professionals out of central cities, it would have done so by now. There is no evidence that it has.

The truth is that we are living at a moment in which the massive outward migration of the affluent that characterized the second half of the twentieth century is coming to an end. And we need to adjust our perceptions of cities, suburbs, and urban mobility as a result.

Much of our perspective on the process of metropolitan settlement dates, whether we realize it or not, from a paper written in 1925 by the University of Chicago sociologist Ernest W. Burgess. It was Burgess who defined four urban/suburban zones of settlement: a central business district; an area of manufacturing just beyond it; then a residential area inhabited by the industrial and immigrant working class; and finally an outer enclave of single-family dwellings.

Burgess was right about the urban America of 1925; he was right about the urban America of 1974. Virtually every city in the country had a downtown, where the commercial life of the metropolis was conducted; it had a factory district just beyond; it had districts of working-class residences just beyond that; and it had residential suburbs for the wealthy and the upper middle class at the far end of the continuum. As a family moved up the economic ladder, it also moved outward from crowded working-class districts to more spacious apartments and, eventually, to a suburban home. The suburbs of Burgess's time bore little resemblance to those at the end of the twentieth century, but the theory still essentially worked. People moved ahead in life by moving farther out.

But in the past decade, in quite a few places, this model has ceased to describe reality. There are still downtown commercial districts, but there are no factory districts lying next to them. There are scarcely any factories at all. These close-in parts of the city, whose few residents Burgess described as dwelling in "submerged regions of poverty, degradation and disease," are increasingly the preserve of the affluent who work in the commercial core. And just as crucially newcomers to America are not settling on the inside and accumulating the resources to move out; they are living in the suburbs from day one.

United States Population by Metropolitan Size/Status, 1980 – 2010

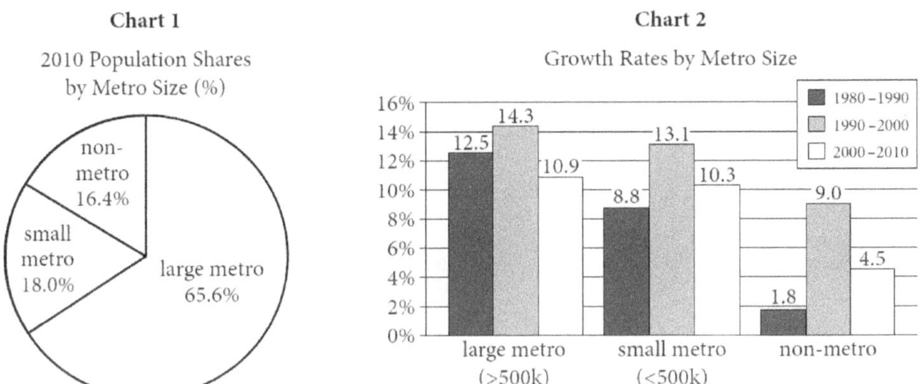

Adapted from William H. Frey, "Population Growth in Metro America since 1980: Putting the Volatile 2000s in Perspective." Published 2012 by Metropolitan Policy Program, Brookings Institution.

Do your SRS for the passage! Reminder of the rules:

(1) You must use the phrase "be like".

(2) You must use no more than two sentences.

(3) Your summary must be comprehensible to a 5-year-old.

(4) Your summary must NOT include any of the words from the passage.

You should have gotten something like this:

Some people moved into the cities and some moved to the suburbs for lots of different reasons. The author be like, "Census data doesn't really help us figure out what's going on."

Now, focus on any opinions you find in this passage (since it's a science passage). Write them down!

The big opinion here is this: "But when it comes to measuring demographic inversion, raw census numbers are an ineffective blunt instrument."

For a science passage, this opinion is really intense. "ineffective blunt instrument" is a massive burn on census data. Why all the hate, Mr. Author?

Well, he gives lots of reasons. The biggest is that, even if you know where people ARE living, you don't know where they WANT to live, if they hope to move soon, why they haven't moved, etc. You know nothing about human motivations, simply by looking at the census.

This opinion, it turns out, will show up in two of the questions for this passage!

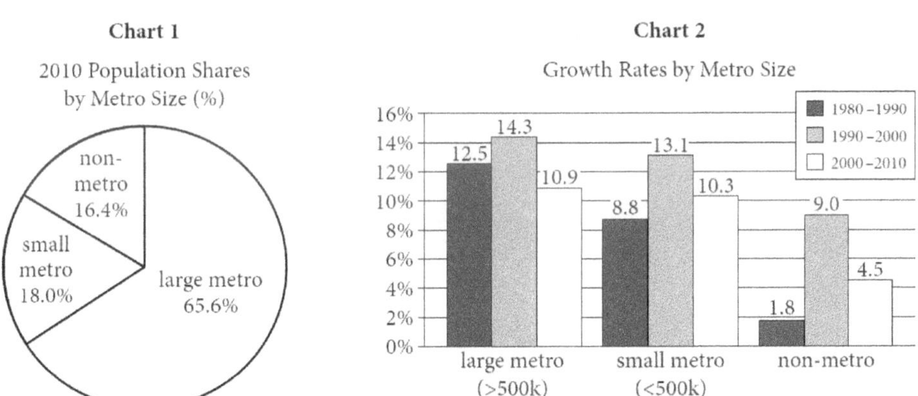

Adapted from William H. Frey, "Population Growth in Metro America since 1980: Putting the Volatile 2000s in Perspective." Published 2012 by Metropolitan Policy Program, Brookings Institution.

Next we do the SRS for each Chart. Proceed.

Chart 1: Here's how many people lived in these three places.

Chart 2: Here's how much population was changing over a couple of years in these three places.

Nothing crazy. Don't pull out numbers. Just get the IDEA of what the Charts are about. Keep it simple!

Question 11

Which choice best summarizes the first paragraph of the passage?

- **(A)** The 2010 census demonstrated a sizeable growth in the number of middle-class families moving into inner cities.
- **(B)** The 2010 census is not a reliable instrument for measuring population trends in American cities.
- **(C)** Population growth and demographic inversion are distinct phenomena, and demographic inversion is evident in many American cities.
- **(D)** Population growth in American cities has been increasing since roughly 2000, while suburban populations have decreased.

Disprove; don't Prove. Pick your answer and your evidence. Challenge yourself to find clear evidence against all the wrong answer choices!

It can help to do a SRS for just the first paragraph here. I'll post a reference answer below.

The SRS for the first paragraph would be something like this:

The author be like, "people live in different places and move around for a variety of reasons that are hard to predict."

Evidence against A: The 2010 census certainly did not turn up evidence of a middle-class stampede to the nation's cities.

Evidence against C: The news was mixed: Some of the larger cities on the East Coast tended to gain population, albeit in small increments. (This shows that there is no clear, consistent demographic inversion.)

But when it comes to measuring demographic inversion, raw census numbers are an ineffective blunt instrument. (Demographic inversion cannot be "evident" if the data that would support it isn't very useful.) If you're not clear on the definition of "evident" look it up! If you don't know what Demographic Inversion is…**read the introductory information above the passage**, oBvIoUsLy.

D is a wild answer. If you picked D, get in touch with me!

B is the answer, and guess what the evidence is?! "But when it comes to measuring demographic inversion, raw census numbers are an ineffective blunt instrument."

It's that quote with the very strong opinion. The author thinks that census data kinda sucks. B says that census data might kind of suck too much to be useful. Et voilà!

It's fun when your focal points really do help. That concept is in your SRS for this passage too (a bit).

Question 12

According to the passage, members of which group moved away from central-city areas in large numbers in the early 2000s?

    (A) The unemployed
    (B) Immigrants
    (C) Young professionals
    (D) African Americans

Answer and evidence! Gimme ittt.

The answer is D. Evidence is "A closer look at the results shows that the most powerful demographic events of the past decade were the movement of African Americans out of central cities…" Note that this was written in 2013 (which I'm sure you read because you always read the introductory info at the top of every passage…), so that "past decade" would be the 2000s.

And yes, I know that the same sentence in the passage goes on to say that "immigrant groups" were settling in the suburbs, too. But, the question is asking who moved "away from central-city areas", it's not asking who moved "to the suburbs".

Those are the small details that make a big difference. You could be moving "to the suburbs" from somewhere else, not central-city.

Question 13

In line 34, "flat" is closest in meaning to

- **(A)** static.
- **(B)** deflated.
- **(C)** featureless.
- **(D)** obscure.

The answer is A.

Keep in mind, for these questions, most of the answer choices will be a **definitional** match, but they won't be a contextual match. You're looking for the **contextual** match, not just definitional!

Question 14

According to the passage, which choice best describes the current financial situation in many major American cities?

- **(A)** Expected tax increases due to demand for public works
- **(B)** Economic hardship due to promises made in past years
- **(C)** Greater overall prosperity due to an increased inner-city tax base
- **(D)** Insufficient revenues due to a decrease in manufacturing

Answer and evidence!

Okay! This one is fun times. There are not one but TWO trick answers here!

D is wrong, but students who pick it usually tell me that they're "sure I saw something about decreased manufacturing somewhere…" The primary place where this is mentioned is in lines 81-84: "There are still downtown commercial districts, but there are no factory districts lying next to them. There are scarcely any factories at all."

What this tells us is that there are fewer factories and factory districts in the inner city/downtown area. What this distinctly does NOT say is that manufacturing decreased. Consider the following:

   » Inner city factories are no longer being used for manufacturing, but we built the same number of factories elsewhere (in suburban or rural areas).

   » We built fewer factories farther out, but each factory is more productive, and therefore manufacturing has increased overall.

   » American cities have insufficient revenues due to some totally other reason that has nothing at all to do with manufacturing.

The list goes on. There are a TON of ways that the quote from the passage can be true while D is still false. Bottom line, D is not clearly supported.

A is also wrong and is the second trick answer. Students who pick A usually point to this quote for evidence: "Some, Chicago prominent among them, simply are not producing enough revenue to support the level of public services to which most of the citizens have grown to feel entitled."

"But Chelsey," they say, "doesn't this suggest that there is, in fact, a demand for public works?" Demand = grown to feel entitled. Public works = public services.

Certainly, dear student, but that's not ALL that A says… A also says "expected tax increases".

I will now tell you a thing about the world: It is VERY-YYYYYYYYYYYY unpopular to raise taxes. Bush Sr. failed to get re-elected in large part because he raised taxes. (Also, he specifically campaigned on NOT raising taxes. That was his big slogan, actually. So…ya, people were pretty annoyed.)

Raising taxes isn't just a thing you can do on a whim. Unless there is some very clear evidence that whatever state or local congress has managed to lay the necessary groundwork to raise taxes (without first getting pitchforked out of office), don't ever expect that taxes will go up in any passage.

And that brings us to B, the correct answer. Here, I want to point out to you how direct and clear and verbatim the SAT can be sometimes.

The question says: Which choice best describes the **current financial situation in many major American cities?**

Now, the part of the passage discussing this is paragraph 2, starting at line 36: "**America's major cities face enormous fiscal problems…**" That's almost word for word! "major American cities" = "America's major cities". "financial" = "fiscal". That should be a huge clue to you. When you see something that is SO directly the same words, you can reasonably assume that that's your key evidence.

So, what does the rest of that sentence say? (It gets better…)

America's major cities face enormous fiscal problems, many of them **the result of public pension obligations they incurred in the more prosperous years of the past two decades.**

B says: Economic hardship due to promises made in past years.

"Economic hardship" = "fiscal problems". "Promises made" = "public pension obligations incurred". "in past years" = "in the more prosper-ous years…"

It is the most word for word question, answer, evidence trio I have ever seen. They won't all be this pretty, but a lot of the SAT will be a bit like this.

When you're keeping it simple, your brain can more easily remember that one paragraph that was talking about some money problems some cities have. From there, it's just a matter of careful reading!

Question 15

Which choice provides the best evidence for the answer to the previous question?

  (A) Lines 36-39 ("America's . . . decades")
  (B) Lines 43-44 ("How . . . not know")
  (C) Lines 44-46 ("What . . . now")
  (D) Lines 48-51 ("The truth . . . end")

This should be simple, now.

The answer is A.

78

Question 16

The passage implies that American cities in 1974

    (A) were witnessing the flight of minority populations to the suburbs.

    (B) had begun to lose their manufacturing sectors.

    (C) had a traditional four-zone structure.

    (D) were already experiencing demographic inversion.

In line with Question 15…I encourage you to look for the part of the passage that is talking about 1974. That's a very easy way to get in the vicinity of the best evidence for this question!

The answer is C. The paragraph that talks about 1974 starts at line 64. In that paragraph, the author is still discussing Burgess's four-zone structure, which was apparently still "right" in 1974.

Again, B here is a distraction for the same reason as before, that bit about decreased manufacturing later in the passage. The SAT is hoping that you'll go based on memory and what you vaguely remember. Obviously, vague rememberings are not going to cut it if you want a perfect score (or anything close). So, real textual evidence, fam!

Question 17

Which choice provides the best evidence for the answer to the previous question?

    (A) Lines 54-57 ("Much . . . Ernest W. Burgess")

    (B) Lines 58-59 ("It was . . . settlement")

    (C) Lines 66-71 ("Virtually . . . continuum")

    (D) Lines 72-75 ("As . . . home")

The answer is C. That quote describes the four-zone structure which the author says was still true for cities in 1974!

Question 18

As used in line 68, "conducted" is closest in meaning to

(A) carried out.
(B) supervised.
(C) regulated.
(D) inhibited.

Look for the contextual match!

Answer is A.

Actually, in this case, the other answers aren't even definitional matches…

Question 19

United States Population by Metropolitan Size/Status, 1980–2010

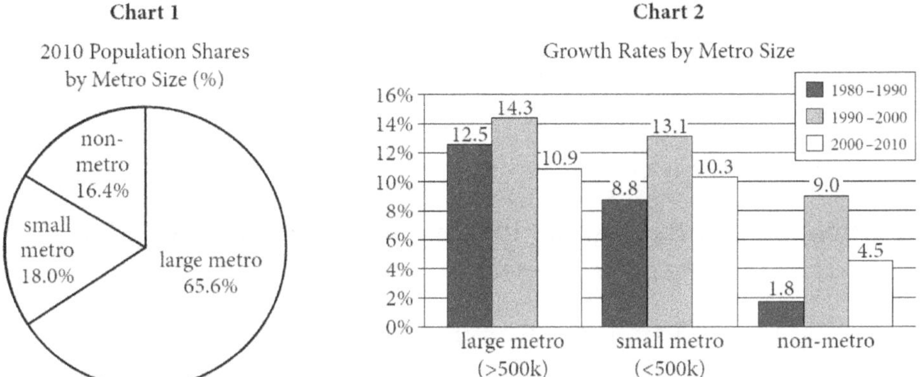

Adapted from William H. Frey, "Population Growth in Metro America since 1980: Putting the Volatile 2000s in Perspective." Published 2012 by Metropolitan Policy Program, Brookings Institution.

The author of the passage would most likely consider the information in chart 1 to be

(A) excellent evidence for the arguments made in the passage.

(B) possibly accurate but too crude to be truly informative.

(C) compelling but lacking in historical information.

(D) representative of a perspective with which the author disagrees.

Answer and evidence!

First thing…I will note here that this question seems to be asking for the author's opinion on something. Did you remember that other ever-so-important opinion we found earlier?

If not, and you want to take a second guess for this question after having a quick look at that opinion again, feel free!

Okay! The answer is B.

Remember, the author isn't a super huge fan of census data. It's just numbers; it doesn't tell us the whole story.

And guess what Chart 1 is? Just numbers. **Basically a census!**

So, the author wouldn't be too keen on Chart 1, but he wouldn't be really against it either (like in D). He just doesn't think it's the best thing ever.

C is a weird one. The SAT put it there because there was discussion of historical stuff in the passage, so maybe you'll get thrown off. If you did, no worries. Just get back up there and try again. The weirdest part of C is that we just don't usually accuse CHARTS of "lacking in historical information". This chart has a date associated with the date. It's from 2010. What possible historical information could you include in here without just pasting in a paragraph next to the chart (in which case, the chart itself still wouldn't have that historical information…).

Question 20

United States Population by Metropolitan Size/Status, 1980–2010

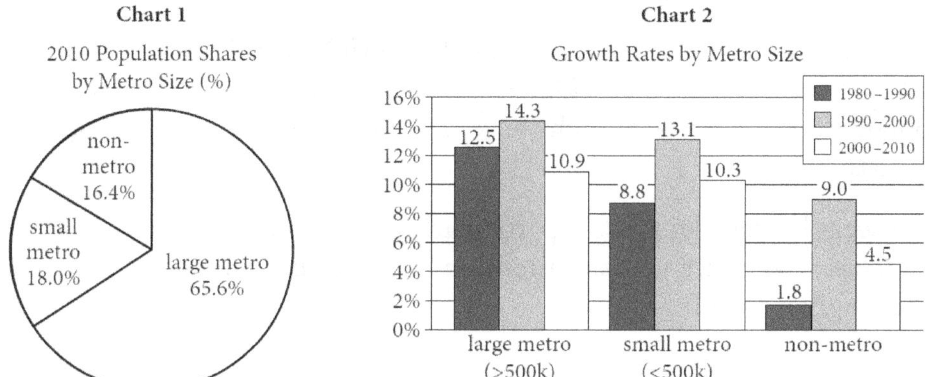

Adapted from William H. Frey, "Population Growth in Metro America since 1980: Putting the Volatile 2000s in Perspective." Published 2012 by Metropolitan Policy Program, Brookings Institution.

According to chart 2, the years 2000–2010 were characterized by

(A) less growth in metropolitan areas of all sizes than had taken place in the 1990s.

(B) more growth in small metropolitan areas than in large metropolitan areas.

(C) a significant decline in the population of small metropolitan areas compared to the 1980s.

(D) roughly equal growth in large metropolitan areas and nonmetropolitan areas.

Answer is A.

The one I really want to pinpoint here is C. Notice that C says "a significant **decline** in the population…"

Now notice that Chart 2 is showing **Growth Rates**. That means that all of those numbers show ONLY growth. There were no declines in population. The growth might have slowed down, but there was still growth.

Answer choices like this are particularly hilarious and worth a good chuckle. Make sure you pay attention to things like that and don't pick the laughable choices!

Question 21

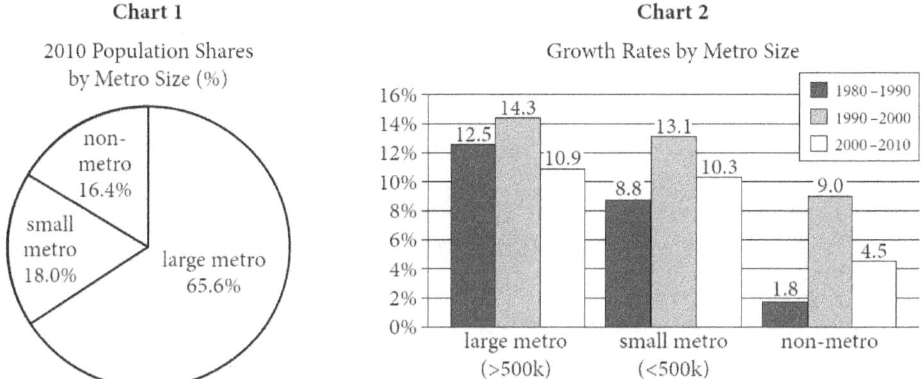

Adapted from William H. Frey, "Population Growth in Metro America since 1980: Putting the Volatile 2000s in Perspective." Published 2012 by Metropolitan Policy Program, Brookings Institution.

Chart 2 suggests which of the following about population change in the 1990s?

(A) Large numbers of people moved from suburban areas to urban areas in the 1990s.

(B) Growth rates fell in smaller metropolitan areas in the 1990s.

(C) Large numbers of people moved from metropolitan areas to nonmetropolitan areas in the 1990s.

(D) The US population as a whole grew more in the 1990s than in the 1980s.

Notice that B says "Growth rates fell" instead of "population declined". That's the correct phrasing IF the bars are going down on this particular graph.

Pick answer! Read the graph carefully.

Answer is D.

Notice that both A and C talk about people **moving** places. This bar graph has no way of showing us where anyone came from or where anyone went to. These could be people moving from out of state, or out of the country. We have no idea. That's **not** the sort of information that bar charts usually hold, AND it speaks to the author's opinion that raw census data kind of sucks; there's not much it can tell us.

Important Note: For science and social science passages, it's important to be keenly aware of the limitations of whatever data. There are tons of questions on the SAT that ask about the charts and graphs, and then give you answers that such data could not possibly hope to prove.

If we wanted to show where people are moving from and to, we would need a completely different survey that asked them for, at least, the zipcodes of their old and new residences. Maybe you could get that data from the post office or something. Regardless, it would look completely different from growth rates...

Science Passage

This passage is adapted from Emily Anthes, *Frankenstein's Cat*. ©2013 by Emily Anthes.

When scientists first learned how to edit the genomes of animals, they began to imagine all the ways they could use this new power. Creating brightly colored novelty pets was not a high priority. Instead, most researchers envisioned far more consequential applications, hoping to create genetically engineered animals that saved human lives. One enterprise is now delivering on this dream. Welcome to the world of "pharming," in which simple genetic tweaks turn animals into living pharmaceutical factories.

Many of the proteins that our cells crank out naturally make for good medicine. Our bodies' own enzymes, hormones, clotting factors, and antibodies are commonly used to treat cancer, diabetes, autoimmune diseases, and more. The trouble is that it's difficult and expensive to make these compounds on an industrial scale, and as a result, patients can face shortages of the medicines they need. Dairy animals, on the other hand, are expert protein producers, their udders swollen with milk. So the creation of the first transgenic animals—first mice, then other species—in the 1980s gave scientists an idea: What if they put the gene for a human antibody or enzyme into a cow, goat, or sheep? If they put gene in just the right place, under the control of the right molecular switch, maybe they could engineer animals that produced healing human proteins in their milk. Then doctors could collect medicine by the bucketful.

Throughout the 1980s and '90s, studies provided proof of principle, as scientists created transgenic mice, sheep, goats, pigs, cattle, and rabbits that did in fact make therapeutic compounds in their milk. At first, this work was merely gee-whiz, scientific geekery, lab-bound thought experiments come true. That all changed with ATryn, a drug produced by the Massachusetts firm GTC Biotherapeutics. ATryn is antithrombin, an anticoagulant that can be used to prevent life-threatening blood clots. The compound, made by our liver cells, plays a key role in keeping our bodies clot-free. It acts as a molecular bouncer, sidling up to clot-forming compounds and escorting them out of the bloodstream. But as many as 1 in 2,000 Americans are born with a genetic mutation that prevents them from making antithrombin. These patients are prone to clots, especially in their legs and lungs, and they are at elevated risk of suffering from fatal complications during surgery and childbirth. Supplemental antithrombin can reduce this risk, and GTC decided to try to manufacture the compound using genetically engineered goats.

To create its special herd of goats, GTC used microinjection, the same technique that produced GloFish and AquAdvantage salmon. The company's scientists took the gene for human antithrombin and injected it directly into fertilized goat eggs. Then they implanted the eggs in the wombs of female goats. When the kids were born, some of them proved to be transgenic, the human gene nestled safely in their cells. The researchers paired the antithrombin gene with a promoter (which is a sequence of DNA that controls gene activity) that is normally active in the goat's mammary glands during milk production. When the transgenic females lactated, the promoter turned the transgene on and the goats' udders filled with milk containing antithrombin. All that was left to do was to collect the milk, and extract and purify the protein. *Et voila*—human medicine! And, for GTC, liquid gold. ATryn hit the market in 2006, becoming the world's first transgenic animal drug. Over the course of a year, the "milking parlors" on GTC's 300-acre farm in Massachusetts can collect more than a kilogram of medicine from a single animal.

Ridiculous Summary time! And keep it Simple.

You should have something like this:

Scientists be like, "Human medicine is hard to make…Let's make it in goats!" The author is nerding out about it and excited.

And…this brings me to one of my favorite bits of hilarity. For some reason, all you students out there are always trying to tell me that every passage in the world has a tone of **"scientific and informative"**.

We're in here reading a passage about how awesome some new roller coaster is, and the author really loved the twists and loops and whatever, and y'all be like, "Oh, this is such a nice, informative brochure about the pleasures of roller coaster riding."

Author: OMG I just LOVE learning about bugs! They're so cooooooooool.

You all: This seems to be a particularly scientific and informative piece of literature about various types of pancrustacean hexapod invertebrates.

My dear dudes and dudettes…**come on!** Not everything is scientific and informative!

Now, here's where this seems to come from: As mentioned before, you have been taught to pretty much hate reading because the books you read in school are usually tediously boring. So, you come to look at all reading as the same: just some information that you don't care about that someone else wants you to know.

Fiction stories? Informative. Exciting new scientific discoveries? Just informative.

NOT EVERYTHING CAN BE SCIENTIFIC AND INFORMATIVE.

So, here's how you can tell. A passage might not be scientific and informative if...

> » It is a fiction or historical passage.
> » The passage uses even one, single exclamation point.
> » There are any opinions of any kind.
> » There is a single emotional word like "awesome", "wow", "impressive", "surprising", or honestly pretty much any other adjective at all.
> » A science passage uses any colloquialisms.
> » A science passage starts talking about "the dream of creating some particular thing".

You have to stop seeing everything as purely boring, emotionless, and "informational".

So, hint hint...the above passage's tone was NOT scientific and informational.

Proceed...

Question 22

The primary purpose of the passage is to

(A) present the background of a medical breakthrough.

(B) evaluate the research that led to a scientific discovery.

(C) summarize the findings of a long-term research project.

(D) explain the development of a branch of scientific study.

This one is fun. Pick your answer and write down your evidence + reasoning!

For this question, a lot of students will pick B or D. The correct answer is A.

Here's what you should learn from this question:

D says that the passage is about the development of a **branch** of scientific study. Ask yourself, what are some **branches** of scientific study that you know about?

Medicine. Astronomy. Paleontology. Those are **branches**. A branch is HUGE. Making medicine in goats is like a sub-sub-twig on the branch of Medicine. So, you can disprove D based on the word "branch", but more importantly, be on the lookout for issues of severity. Is an opinion weak or severe (like the guy who hated census data)? Is some data weak or powerful? Is a branch a big thing or a small thing? Etc. The size and weight of a single word can make the difference.

For B, it's a little tougher. At first glance, B and A look nearly identical (which is obviously the point, hopefully you know the SAT well enough by now!). "Background" and "research that led to something" are kind of the same thing. A "medical breakthrough" could be considered a "scientific discovery", so that's also pretty similar.

What about "present" vs "evaluate"? Here we have a bigger difference, so we'll focus our efforts. And again here we have an issue of intensity. When you "evaluate" something, you've got criticisms, praise, maybe you rank things or set grades for various aspects of the thing. You evaluate workers at your company. You evaluate a course to tell the teacher if it was good or if it sucked. Your teacher evaluates your essay to tell you if it was good or…sucked (lol). Evaluations can be hefty.

Presentations are just like, "Here is some information." It's a much softer word.

So, are we ranking and grading the research in this passage, or is the author just telling us about it? Well, you already know it's A, but that's the question you would ask yourself on the next test!

Question 23

The author's attitude toward pharming is best described as one of

- **(A)** apprehension.
- **(B)** ambivalence.
- **(C)** appreciation.
- **(D)** astonishment.

Remember that the tone is NOT "scientific and informative". Answer the question, write down your thinking, then read on!

This is a vocab thing, so…**do Vocab Synapse!** It's free. If you're not doing it yet, then do you even actually want a good SAT score? Don't kid yourself. Vocab takes time to train. It takes months and years. You have weeks. Get it together!

If you are doing your Synapse, good. I hope you're managing to get 30 points by now!

The answer here is A. The most common wrong answer is D. Again here we have an issue of severity. "Astonishment" is a much more intense emotion. It's like HUGE shock, like you simply cannot possibly believe that a thing is true.

This author is telling us all about the science that led to the breakthrough, remember? So, she probably isn't sitting there thinking, "I cannot possibly believe this." She saw it coming; she knew what they were trying to accomplish.

She's definitely excited that they did it, but she's not completely and totally shocked and speechless or anything like that.

If you picked A, my guess is that you just didn't know the words. Go learn all these four definitions right now!

And a very important note for B: The SAT **loves** the word "ambivalence" because you all never use that word correctly. If you see "ambivalent" anywhere…it's a trap!

Ambivalent means that you have clear positive AND negative feelings about a thing. Ambivalent does not mean indifferent and opinion-less, or undecided, or anything like that.

Indifferent: Eh, idk what I want to eat.
Ambivalent: I really want to eat Chipotle because it's delish, but the spices sometimes give me heartburn… (Clear positive, clear negative, BOTH)

Deeply internalize the meaning of ambivalent so that you can get that question right on your next SAT.

Question 24

As used in line 20, "expert" most nearly means

    (A) knowledgeable.

    (B) professional.

    (C) capable.

    (D) trained.

Remember, you're looking for a contextual match, not just a definitional one. Expert CAN mean all four of the words above. But, are these goats super "knowledgeable" at making milk? Are they "professionals" at it? Did they need to be "trained" to make milk? No, that would be weird.

Answer is C.

Question 25

What does the author suggest about the transgenic studies done in the 1980s and 1990s?

- **(A)** They were limited by the expensive nature of animal research.
- **(B)** They were not expected to yield products ready for human use.
- **(C)** They were completed when an anticoagulant compound was identified.
- **(D)** They focused only on the molecular properties of cows, goats, and sheep.

Answer and evidence, obv!

Remember, when a question gives you all the clues for where to look in the passage…you should go look in that place. The question mentions "**transgenic studies** done in the **1980s and 1990s**". Paragraph 3 starts with, "Throughout the **1980s and '90s, studies** provided proof of principle, as scientists created **transgenic** mice, sheep, goats, pigs, cattle, and rabbits…" (Lines 31-33)

So, if you're pulling evidence from somewhere else…quit it.

Any evidence for A comes from line 17, which is not associated with the studies in the 80s and 90s.

D is obviously wrong; they looked at lots of animals. You can disprove D using the word "only".

Then it's down to B and C. C is the clever trick answer here, and it speaks to an important point about implications.

The SAT is always asking what the passage "implies" or what the author "suggests", etc. When they say "implies" and "suggests", they basically are just asking for what's stated in the passage. Don't think of "implies" as your moment to shine with all your ridiculous Mental Gymnastics again! It ain't time for that!!

You're looking for something unarguable and clearly supported in the passage. The issue with C is that it says the transgenic studies were "completed". The passage certainly says that things "changed" with ATryn. But, that doesn't mean that all those scientists were like, "Oh gosh, someone invented a thing. I guess I will suddenly abandon all my research of the past two decades and do something else with my life…"

Science goes on. Scientists try to improve on whatever was invented. Somebody has to make ATryn version 2.0 and 6.0.

So, there's no reason to believe that all the scientists suddenly quit working. But, the quote about "gee-whiz, scientific geekery" does tell us that people didn't think anything was going to come out of that research. When you describe something like that, it means that it's sort of a pipe dream.

At some point, you might start to feel that in three weeks, you won't have the time to gain enough knowledge about the world to get questions like this. In a sense, that's true. That's why we're building all the other skills up. You can still get very few questions wrong and get a 1500 (though basically none in math).

But, I want to reiterate the skill of asking yourself, "What would __________ look like?"

If you said, "I just did a pull up!", and your friend said, "gee whiz", then you **know** that your friend is probably impressed and **surprised**. Surprise only happens when you didn't think something would happen. So, you can use what you know to arrive at the same conclusions.

Trust what you KNOW. Don't worry about what you don't know. On test day, you factually cannot change what you don't know at that moment in time. You must rely on the skills you have and trust yourself. Doubting yourself cannot possibly help anyone.

Question 26

Evidence time!

Prior question: What does the author suggest about the transgenic studies done in the 1980s and 1990s?
Answer: They were not expected to yield products ready for human use.

Which choice provides the best evidence for the answer to the previous question?

- **(A)** Lines 16-19 ("The trouble . . . need")
- **(B)** Lines 25-29 ("If they . . . milk")
- **(C)** Lines 35-36 ("At first . . . true")
- **(D)** Lines 37-40 ("That all . . . clots")

The answer is C. I want to use this question to reinforce my rule of NEVER answering this paired question type together.

Answer choice A from question 25: They were limited by the **expensive** nature of animal research.
Pairs perfectly with A from 26: "The trouble is that it's difficult and **expensive to make** these compounds on an industrial scale, and as a result, patients can face shortages of the medicines they need."

BUT! A isn't the answer to the question in 25.

C from 25: They were completed when an **anticoagulant** compound was identified.
Pairs nicely with D from 26: "That all changed with ATryn, a drug produced by the Massachusetts firm GTC Biotherapeutics. ATryn is antithrombin, an **anticoagulant** that can be used to prevent life-threatening blood clots."

Remember, discovery of one thing doesn't mean that all other research shuts down. But, there does seem to be reasonable support for C… It's very misleading, and that's the whole point.

You can even get fooled by the following:

Answer D from 25: They focused only on the molecular properties of cows, goats, and sheep.
Evidence B from 26: "*What if they put the gene for a human antibody or enzyme into a cow, goat, or sheep?* If they put the gene in just the right place, under the control of the right molecular switch, maybe they could engineer animals that produced healing human proteins in their milk."

The italicized sentence isn't part of the quote given in B, but when you go looking at line 25, you're bound to see the words "cow, goat, or sheep" close by.

These are the sorts of things the SAT is relying on. This is how they trick you. But, tricks like that are SO easy to avoid! Just physically cover up the evidence questions while reading the initial question and…Presto! Their trick no longer works.

Question 27

According to the passage, which of the following is true of antithrombin?

(A) It reduces compounds that lead to blood clots.
(B) It stems from a genetic mutation that is rare in humans.
(C) It is a sequence of DNA known as a promoter.
(D) It occurs naturally in goats' mammary glands.

Answer + evidence! Write it down.

Small note: You know that antithrombin gets introduced in the third paragraph. So, don't go looking for an answer in the first or second paragraphs, obviously. That's part of using your time wisely. Know the layout of the passages.

I know you all are in love with annotating every single word on a page, and you probably don't need me to lecture you again on how idiotic it is to underline 85% of a passage… One thing you can make note of, though, is **a big change or introduction**. If the passage is all about one thing, and then suddenly it shifts, then you should categorize the passage into "stuff that came before that shift" and "stuff that came after".

Personally, I do this in my head. I'm capable of that because I read a LOT of books, including a lot of non-fiction, science journals, etc. In three weeks, you might not get to that level (but you should still try), but you can make a small note for big changes in the passage. You can even just draw a big line at that point.

Okay! The answer is A. The introduction to ATryn starts at line 38, and the evidence we want (which you should have written down on your paper) is in the area of lines 40-44: "The compound, made by our liver cells, plays a key role in keeping our bodies clot-free. It acts as a molecular bouncer, **sidling up to clot-forming compounds and escorting them out of the bloodstream**."

Some students miss this one because the evidence is written in as a personification/metaphor thing. If you got it wrong, practice disproving whichever answer choice you picked!

Question 28

Prior Question:

According to the passage, which of the following is true of antithrombin?

    (A) It reduces compounds that lead to blood clots.

    (B) It stems from a genetic mutation that is rare in humans.

    (C) It is a sequence of DNA known as a promoter.

    (D) It occurs naturally in goats' mammary glands.

Current Question:

Which choice provides the best evidence for the answer to the previous question?

    (A) Lines 12-16 ("Many . . . more")

    (B) Lines 42-44 ("It acts . . . bloodstream")

    (C) Lines 44-46 ("But as . . . antithrombin")

    (D) Lines 62-65 ("The researchers . . . production")

And the answer is B, of course.

And we have the trick pair B + C. Also the trick pair D + D. And, fun stuff, we have the pair C + D. D is trick evidence for not one but TWO answers to the prior question!

Question 29

Which of the following does the author suggest about the "female goats" mentioned in line 59?

(A) They secreted antithrombin in their milk after giving birth.

(B) Some of their kids were not born with the antithrombin gene.

(C) They were the first animals to receive microinjections.

(D) Their cells already contained genes usually found in humans.

Answer and evidence written down on your paper!

This question is epic, and it brings up a smaller thing that you can look for. You've learned all the big rules and tips, so you can start to look for more nuanced tricks and traps in the SAT!

So, the answer is B. Most students who get this wrong pick A. Time to analyze.

A big chunk from the passage:

The company's scientists took the gene for human antithrombin and injected it directly into fertilized goat eggs. Then they implanted the eggs in the wombs of **female goats**. When the kids were born, some of them proved to be transgenic, the human gene nestled safely in their cells. The researchers paired the antithrombin gene with a promoter (which is a sequence of DNA that controls gene activity) that is normally active in the goat's mammary glands during milk production. When the transgenic females lactated, the promoter turned the transgene on and the goats' udders filled with milk containing antithrombin.

The bolded "female goats" are the ones we're interested in; those are the ones in line 59. Those are also the first ones. So, they edited the genes in some goat eggs, stuck them in a normal goat who becomes the **momma goat**, and then the momma goat had **babies**.

When the **babies** come out, some of them have the antithrombin gene. Those ones get some injections of "promoter" which just kick-starts the antithrombin stuff.

Now we get to this sentence: "When the **transgenic females** lactated, the promoter turned the transgene on and the goats' udders filled with milk containing antithrombin."

Which goats are the "transgenic females"? The **momma goat** or the **baby goats** (who obviously grow up at some point).

It's the baby goats; those are the ones that have the transgene. The momma goat was just a normal goat, nothing special. She carried the gene **in her womb**, but not in her own genes.

So, momma goat did not have any antithrombin milk. The **baby goats** grew up, had their own babies, and then made antithrombin milk.

Now, the question asks about the "female goats" in line 59. Here's the passage again:

The company's scientists took the gene for human antithrombin and injected it directly into fertilized goat eggs. Then they implanted the eggs in the wombs of **female goats**. When the kids were born, some of them proved to be transgenic, the human gene nestled safely in their cells. The researchers paired the antithrombin gene with a promoter (which is a sequence of DNA that controls gene activity) that is normally active in the goat's mammary glands during milk production. When the **transgenic females** lactated, the promoter turned the transgene on and the goats' udders filled with milk containing antithrombin.

Which goats are the "female goats"? The mommas or the babies?

Those ones are the momma goats. That sentence says that those goats got the implanted, gene-edited eggs.

So, the evidence that "proves" answer choice A…actually pertains to the grown up baby goats, NOT to the goats mentioned in line 59.

SAT Trick: The SAT does this a lot. They like to introduce two "characters" very close together so that you'll get confused about which is which.

Solution: As much as I make fun of annotating things, THIS is a good time to make small notes. If there are ever several characters or things introduced close together, just make sure that you know what every pronoun refers to. Who is "her" talking about? Which one is "it"? Which are the "female goats" and which are the "transgenic females"? Pronouns and referential names (anything that isn't directly naming the thing/person) should be clarified, by you, before moving on.

Note: If you feel like all this science is above your head, just go to Google, search "gene editing", and read the first 4 things that come up. You'll be fine.

You don't need to know everything, but you should expose yourself to the big ideas in the world today. You should be able to name several different environmentally friendly energy options that are being explored. You should know that there are a few general types of rock. You should know that people don't like taxes. You should know that people lie to preserve social graces. You should know that gene editing is a thing. You should know that AI is a thing and people like to worry about it a lot. There are just big ticket items that you want to be aware of.

The way you learn all those things is…you guessed it, reading.

Question 30

The most likely purpose of the parenthetical information in lines 63–64 is to

(A) illustrate an abstract concept.

(B) describe a new hypothesis.

(C) clarify a claim.

(D) define a term.

Most students get this one right. Answer is D.

If you picked A…don't just go picking "abstract concept" because you think everything is abstract! Not everything is abstract. Abstract is the opposite of "concrete". It doesn't just mean "something I'm having a hard time understanding". lol

Question 31

The phrase "liquid gold" (line 71) most directly suggests that

(A) GTC has invested a great deal of money in the microinjection technique.

(B) GTC's milking parlors have significantly increased milk production.

(C) transgenic goats will soon be a valuable asset for dairy farmers.

(D) ATryn has proved to be a financially beneficial product for GTC.

Answer is D. Students often pick A here. If you did, don't worry. But, you need to think about the directionality and common sense over here. "Gold" probably clued you in that this is about money, and from there you can figure out what specific thing is "liquid gold" here.

It's the milk that GTC is producing. If you are producing gold…are you going to be super poor or super rich? Rich. It doesn't really matter if you had to invest a lot of money upfront (and we have no evidence that they did). You're still going to make a lot of money, for sure.

Don't do mental gymnastics! Don't think, "well, if it produces them a lot of money, then they probably would increase the milk production, so maybe it's B…" No. That's jumping through hoops.

Anyways, "liquid gold" or "______ gold" is a pretty common phrase that you should be aware of. Comedy gold. Culinary gold. Academic gold. It just means that the thing is super duper good.

Dual Passages

Passage 1

Passage 1 is adapted from Edmund Burke, *Reflections on the Revolution in France*. Originally published in 1790. Passage 2 is adapted from Thomas Paine, *Rights of Man*. Originally published in 1791.

To avoid . . . the evils of inconstancy and versatility, ten thousand times worse than those of obstinacy and the blindest prejudice, we have consecrated the state, that no man should approach to look into its defects or corruptions but with due caution; that he should never dream of beginning its reformation by its subversion; that he should approach to the faults of the state as to the wounds of a father, with pious awe and trembling solicitude. By this wise prejudice we are taught to look with horror on those children of their country who are prompt rashly to hack that aged parent in pieces, and put him into the kettle of magicians, in hopes that by their poisonous weeds, and wild incantations, they may regenerate the paternal constitution, and renovate their father's life.

Society is indeed a contract. Subordinate contracts for objects of mere occasional interest may be dissolved at pleasure—but the state ought not to be considered as nothing better than a partnership agreement in a trade of pepper and coffee, calico or tobacco, or some other such low concern, to be taken up for a little temporary interest, and to be dissolved by the fancy of the parties. It is to be looked on with other reverence; because it is not a partnership in things subservient only to the gross animal existence of a temporary and perishable nature. It is a partnership in all science; a partnership in all art; a partnership in every virtue, and in all perfection. As the ends of such a partnership cannot be obtained in many generations, it becomes a partnership not only between those who are living, but between those who are living, those who are dead, and those who are to be born. . . . The municipal corporations of that universal kingdom are not morally at liberty at their pleasure, and on their speculations of a contingent improvement, wholly to separate and tear asunder the bands of their subordinate community, and to dissolve it into an unsocial, uncivil, unconnected chaos of elementary principles.

Once you finish, go ahead and attempt your SRS!

HAHA. That pretty much totally sucked, didn't it? Almost all of my students end up somewhere between "no idea" and "um…contracts?"

Grammar and Historical Context

First paragraph

So, if you get a passage like this on your real SAT, what should you do? Jump into Aggressive Grammar Mode, and then General Knowledge Mode. We're going to spend a LOT of time on this passage, so buckle up!

Here's your grammar crash course review:

English is made up of phrases and clauses. It has nouns, verbs, and modifiers. Some things perform the action of the verb and other things get acted on. If you can figure out what the action is, who's doing it, and why, then you'll be in really good shape. The end.

So, for starters, the following is all one sentence. Find the main verb (that's the verb NOT in any modifying clauses).

To avoid . . . the evils of inconstancy and versatility, ten thousand times worse than those of obstinacy and the blindest prejudice, we have consecrated the state, that no man should approach to look into its defects or corruptions but with due caution; that he should never dream of beginning its reformation by its subversion; that he should approach to the faults of the state as to the wounds of a father, with pious awe and trembling solicitude.

The main verb is "have consecrated". And who is doing the consecrating?

"We" are. So, "we have consecrated…" What is the direct object?

The state.

We have consecrated the state. That's the core of our sentence. Literally all the rest of it is just explaining why "we" did that.

Now, if you don't know what "consecrated" means, say it with me... DO YOUR VOCAB SYNAPSE.

Also, look it up, make a flashcard, learn the word. It's a common enough word. You should know it.

So, this sentence basically says that we made the state holy/sacred, that's just a fancy way of saying that "the state" is super important and special and stuff. Also, "the state" is an older term for "the government". So, "we made the government sacred". That right there tells you like 90% of what this passage is about. This dude thinks that the government is super sacred and important and shouldn't be messed with.

From there, we can start to look at some of the other pieces.

~Try to find all of the prepositional phrases in this sentence.

To avoid . . . the evils of inconstancy and versatility, ten thousand times worse than those of obstinacy and the blindest prejudice, we have consecrated the state, that no man should approach to look into its defects or corruptions but with due caution; that he should never dream of beginning its reformation by its subversion; that he should approach to the faults of the state as to the wounds of a father, with pious awe and trembling solicitude.

These are the prepositional phrases (if you need to learn more about those, check out my grammar crash course):

To avoid . . . the evils **[of inconstancy and versatility]**, ten thousand times worse than those **[of obstinacy and the blindest prejudice]**, we have consecrated the state, that no man should approach to look **[into its defects or corruptions]** but **[with due caution]**; that he should never dream **[of beginning its reformation]** **[by its subversion]**; that he should approach **[to the faults]** **[of the state]** as **[to the wounds]** **[of a father]**, **[with pious awe and trembling solicitude]**.

Prepositional phrases are, as you can see, very common.

~Now go through and try to figure out what each prepositional phrase modifies.

Here are the answers:

To avoid . . . the evils [of inconstancy and versatility] **(modifies "the evils")**, ten thousand times worse than those [of obstinacy and the blindest prejudice] **(modifies "those" which refers to "the evils")**, we have consecrated the state, that no man should approach to look [into its defects or corruptions] **(modifies "to look)** but [with due caution] **(modifies "approach")**; that he should never dream [of beginning its reformation] **(modifies "dream")** [by its subversion] **(modifies "beginning")**; that he should approach [to the faults] **(modifies "approach")** [of the state] **(modifies "faults")** as [to the wounds] **(modifies "approach")** [of a father] **(modifies "wounds")**, [with pious awe and trembling solicitude] **(modifies "approach")**.

~Now find all infinitives.

To avoid . . . the evils of inconstancy and versatility, ten thousand times worse than those of obstinacy and the blindest prejudice, we have consecrated the state, that no man should approach to look into its defects or corruptions but with due caution; that he should never dream of beginning its reformation by its subversion; that he should approach to the faults of the state as to the wounds of a father, with pious awe and trembling solicitude.

Only two.

[To avoid . . . the evils of inconstancy and versatility, ten thousand times worse than those of obstinacy and the blindest prejudice], we have consecrated the state, that no man should approach **[to look]** into its defects or corruptions but with due caution; that he should never dream of beginning its reformation by its subversion; that he should approach to the faults of the state as to the wounds of a father, with pious awe and trembling solicitude.

If you're getting these wrong, head over to the grammar crash course and get up to speed with core grammar rules.

~What do those two infinitives modify?

[To avoid . . . the evils of inconstancy and versatility, ten thousand times worse than those of obstinacy and the blindest prejudice] **(modifies "have consecrated")**, we have consecrated the state, that no man should approach [to look] **(modifies "approach")** into its defects or corruptions but with due caution; that he should never dream of beginning its reformation by its subversion; that he should approach to the faults of the state as to the wounds of a father, with pious awe and trembling solicitude.

Okay, at this point we have a lot of information.

Why did we make the government sacred/holy? So that we can avoid these various "evils". Which evils? The evils of inconstancy and versatility. What do those words mean? **Go do more vocab synapse!** And also look them up, make flash cards, etc. How bad are inconstancy and versatility? WAY worse than obstinacy and blind prejudice.

So, now we're getting a picture of what the author likes, doesn't like, thinks is good, thinks is terrible, etc.

Next, we do clauses!

~Find all clauses (noun, adjective, and adverb) and highlight them.

To avoid . . . the evils of inconstancy and versatility, ten thousand times worse than those of obstinacy and the blindest prejudice, we have consecrated the state, that no man should approach to look into its defects or corruptions but with due caution; that he should never dream of beginning its reformation by its subversion; that he should approach to the faults of the state as to the wounds of a father, with pious awe and trembling solicitude.

Also, in older English, when people use the word "that" as it's used here, they mean "so that". Basically, if a regular "that" doesn't seem to make sense, try "so that" and see if that makes sense.

Also also! In older English, "should" often really means "would".

I'll edit those things in the answer below:

To avoid . . . the evils of inconstancy and versatility, ten thousand times worse than those of obstinacy and the blindest prejudice, **[we have consecrated the state]** (main clause), **[SO that no man WOULD approach to look into its defects or corruptions but with due caution]; [SO that he WOULD never dream of beginning its reformation by its subversion]; [SO that he WOULD approach to the faults of the state as to the wounds of a father, with pious awe and trembling solicitude].**

~And now figure out what each of the non-main clauses modifies!

To avoid . . . the evils of inconstancy and versatility, ten thousand times worse than those of obstinacy and the blindest prejudice, [we have consecrated the state] (main clause), [so that no man would approach to look into its defects or corruptions but with due caution] **(modifies "have consecrated")**; [so that he would never dream of beginning its reformation by its subversion] **(modifies "have consecrated")**; [so that he would approach to the faults of the state as to the wounds of a father, with pious awe and trembling solicitude] **(modifies "have consecrated")**.

And now we know a lot more reasons for why we made the state sacred/holy. When you make something sacred, you can't just go and destroy it willy nilly, or even change it in any way. It's sacred; it's godly. You can't just edit the Bible or the Quran. People live and die protecting holy lands, holy spots. It's a really big deal.

For many people, the government is, if not "holy", at least very important. Lots of people don't want you to JUST change stuff. They don't take changes lightly. That's why Congress is so often gridlocked. That's why the legislative branch is slow to get things done. No matter what change you suggest, someone, somewhere thinks it's a bad idea. Actually a lot of someones in a lot of somewheres REALLY do not want you to change whatever thing you want to change.

Sometimes that's because it benefits them, personally, like various subsidies or grants or programs. Sometimes it's because they want to uphold some ideals. Whatever the reason, this is a general worldly thing you should understand.

If you're not very familiar with politics at all, go read what the right, the left, the center, the libertarians, the greens, and everyone else have to say about some of the biggest issues out there today. Don't look at what the left says that the right says, or vice versa. They will obviously both demonize the other.

Go and actually look at what normal, kind, caring people on both sides believe. Ask Google what's so bad/good about gun control, what's so good/bad about pro-life, why should we (or shouldn't we) lower the drinking and voting ages, and what should we do about illegal immigration. Look at all the major issues.

How do you know if you're reading a carefully considered opinion or just another page of propaganda for the Reds or the Blues? Genuine opinions often don't align perfectly with either side. Genuine opinions almost always end up in the middle because there are tons of gray areas.

Once you've done that, come back, and let's continue.

~Write out all the things that Burke doesn't want to have happen (aka, all the reasons why we had to make the government holy/sacred). SIMPLIFY what Dudeface McGee over here is saying, obviously. Ain't nobody got time for this density...

To avoid . . . the evils of inconstancy and versatility, ten thousand times worse than those of obstinacy and the blindest prejudice, we have consecrated the state, that no man should approach to look into its defects or corruptions but with due caution; that he should never dream of beginning its reformation by its subversion; that he should approach to the faults of the state as to the wounds of a father, with pious awe and trembling solicitude.

Answer: He doesn't want people to come up in here and be like, "this government sucks, let's tear it down and build a new one!"

That's basically it. Now, let's get some context. Which group of people had, very recently, said, "this government sucks, let's tear it down and build a new one!" (If you don't know when this passage was written... then I have caught you red handed! Go read the intro informationnn-nnn.)

Hopefully you got this one right. It was the American colonists!

And not only did they dislike their prior government, they also succeeded in overthrowing it! Happy Birthday US.

So, the American Revolution ended in 1783, just 8 years prior to the publication of this passage.

You: But Chelsey, I didn't know I needed to know DATES for the SAT! I hate history!

Me: You should probably know at least the year 1776 (Declaration of Independence). If you know that year, then you can imagine the American Revolution would either have been completed or **maybe** still going. Either way, the context is basically the same. Burke has seen what happens when people don't like a government, and he doesn't want that to happen to his government (probably because he is in some way connected to or benefitted by his government, though we don't know that for sure.) War is generally seen as bad.

So, this isn't about knowing a bunch of dates, but there are common knowledge things that you should be aware of just because you're a human being, and if you are aware of those things, they can only help you!

Now, what you may not know is that the French Revolution was also ongoing at this time, and it was about to get a whole lot worse in the very next year after Burke's essay. So, there are also a bunch of people looking at the French government and saying, "This sucks; let's overthrow it." Not Burke's idea of a good time. Not usually anyone's idea of a good time.

We DO know the title of Burke's passage is *Reflections on the Revolution in France*. So, again, you don't have to know dates; you can still get the vague context here.

So, he says things like, don't try to "reform" the government by subverting it, and, treat the government like a wounded father. You wouldn't just kill your dad and overthrow him, would you?! So, don't do that to the government either.

This is what it looks like to analyze a passage. This is how you can think through passages on your own. It takes practice, but you can do it.

Ask yourself a few things:

>> **Are there any historical events I know about that happened around this time?** (If not, that's fine.)

>> **Are there any general historical things that might be pertinent to this passage?** (Think war in general, governmental overthrow in general, fighting for human rights in general. Even if you don't know specific events, you know how history has generally gone. People fight for usually stupid but sometimes decent reasons. People oppress other people. Oppressed people always rise up and overthrow their oppressors. Some people are always poor; some are always rich. Wealth and class disparities always create problems and strife. Governments always end up overreaching their power. Things like that are just general knowledge about human nature.)

>> **Does the author seem to like or dislike particular things? Which things?** (Remember, the Historical passages are all about opinions. Opinions will probably be everywhere.)

So, from a bit of grammatical analysis and historical knowledge (or just an understanding of human nature and how history always goes) we have figured out that this guy likes the government and wants it to stay NOT overthrown.

Positive/Negative whole passage

With that third question alone (what does the author like/dislike), we can arrive at a similar conclusion. Let's look at the whole passage for a minute.

~See if you can find all the major nouns. What I mean by this is all the nouns that are subjects or direct objects, **not** the nouns that are objects of prepositions. (Again, if you're lost, do the grammar crash course!)

Here are the big ones I came up with:

> » The state
> » Man (this is the general man whom the author doesn't want doing all that stuff.)
> » Those children (this is technically part of a prepositional phrase, but "horror" shows a clear opinion associated with these peeps.)
> » That aged parent
> » Society (which is a contract) (line 17)
> » Subordinate contracts
> » Partnerships (in science, art, virtue, and perfection) (lines 28-29)
> » The municipal corporations (look up municipal if you don't know it) (line 34)
> » The bands (of their subordinate community) (line 38)

~When Burke mentions "that aged parent", what is he referencing?

He's referring to the government. He talks about treating the government like a father earlier. So, we can combine "the state" with "that aged parent".

~Now go through and try to figure out how Burke feels about these nouns. First, just look for the STRONGLY positive or negative ones.

- » Government
- » Man (this is the general man whom the author doesn't want doing all that stuff.)
- » Those children (line 11)
- » Society (which is a contract) (line 17)
- » Subordinate contracts
- » Partnerships (in science, art, virtue, and perfection) (lines 28-29)
- » The municipal corporations (look up municipal if you don't know it) (line 34)
- » The bands (of their subordinate community) (line 38)

» Government **(super positive, obv. That's the whole point of the passage.)**

» Man (this is the general man whom the author doesn't want doing all that stuff.) **(Negative. This is the generic guy who's trying to tear down Burke's precious government, like a savage! lol)**

» Those children (line 11) **(SUPER negative. We look on these "children" with horror. Btw, he doesn't mean like infants and toddlers. He's just being insulting by calling, for example, the people who put on the American Revolution "children".)**

» Society (which is a contract) (line 17) **(uncertain, maybe neutral or positive.)**

» Subordinate contracts **(Negative. He calls them subordinate and uses other phrases like "mere occasional interest" or "some other such low concern".)**

» Partnerships (in science, art, virtue, and perfection) (lines 28-29) **(These partnerships describe what the government is. He likes government!)**

» The municipal corporations (look up municipal if you don't know it) (line 34) **(Negative. He's telling them that they have no right to try to tear apart everything that is good in the world (aka government…))**

» The bands (of their subordinate community) (line 38) **(Positive. The word "bands" means the stuff that ties the community together, aka government again!)**

So, things that are good: The government, society (when it is a good contract and run by the government), partnerships in awesome things (which the government is), and the (governmental) bands that tie together a community.

Things that are bad: People who try to tear down the government, "children" who try to overthrow their government, contracts and partnerships in lowly, commoner things like food and housing, and municipal corporations (if they try to separate from the government).

Even simpler: Government good. Anti-government bad.

And that, my friends, is 80% of the SRS for this passage.

Now, here you say, "But Chelsey, that took forever! I don't have that much time on the test." And I say, "Yes, obviously. And everyone who achieves sub-4-minute mile times also took the time to slowly, painstakingly learn how to walk, first. You don't JUST be good at this stuff. I'm here to show you what you should practice, tricks you can use, approaches that will work. Then you have to practice them!"

So, now it's time to practice. Go through the rest of the sentences in this passage, identify prepositional phrases, infinitives, modifying clauses, etc. and write out what you think they modify. Use that to build your understanding of the connectedness of language in writing. Figure out what the rest of the passage is saying, using that 80% of the SRS we have so far.

You WILL gain speed with this. All of this work won't be necessary for every passage forever, nor will it be necessary on your real SAT. But, practicing slowly and painstakingly at first will lead to greater success later.

Second Paragraph

Society is indeed a contract. Subordinate contracts for objects of mere occasional interest may be dissolved at pleasure—but the state ought not to be considered as nothing better than a partnership agreement in a trade of pepper and coffee, calico or tobacco, or some other such low concern, to be taken up for a little temporary interest, and to be dissolved by the fancy of the parties. It is to be looked on with other reverence; because it is not a partnership in things subservient only to the gross animal existence of a temporary and perishable nature. It is a partnership in all science; a partnership in all art; a partnership in every virtue, and in all perfection.

A few questions about these "contracts":

1. What are the "objects of mere occasional interest" Burke is referencing?
2. What is the "gross animal existence"?
3. What is the government NOT about? What is the government about?

Answers:

1. Pepper, coffee, calico, tobacco (and other such low concerns, lol)
2. Just surviving, like animals.
3. Not about pepper, coffee, calico, and tobacco. The government IS about science, art, virtue, and all perfection. (Again, all this is according to Burke.)

Burke is making a distinction here between two types of contracts: the lowly contracts made by commoners who are only interested in eating food and living (how awful!) and the very high and lofty contracts of the government, which is interested in pursuits like science, art, and virtue.

If you can't feel the pompousness in this…you have your work cut out for you! It's okay though, most students don't see it at first. But, "gross animal existence" should clue you in. That sounds like a pretty **strong** opinion! Animals are interested in surviving long enough to reproduce. To do that, they need shelter, food, and a mate. Humans are capable of higher pursuits like art and science, sure, but we also need food and shelter…

Here, Burke is insulting people for only being interested in eating food and living in a house, which is a pretty silly insult. It's also a pretty common one that is used to show how people are incapable of pursuing the right things and so the educated few (government) must make decisions for the masses; they can't make the right choices themselves.

Is the government interested in science and art? Probably. Are they also probably concerned about food? Yes. Do the people in Burke's government live in houses? Yes. So, his argument really falls apart here. It's just trash talk, at this point. His important takeaway is, "Look how perfect and special the government is. It's better than you; you're stupid." Which leads us right back to…"don't change the government or overthrow it!"

Finding the Thesis

So, before I said that we have 80% of the SRS just from the positives and negatives, and we've read and analyzed the entire passage, now. Where's the other 20% of the SRS? It comes from the thesis.

Tip for finding theses: The thesis statement of a passage can come anywhere in that passage. Most often, it comes at the very beginning or the very end, but not always. The thesis is the same as the conclusion; it should be the big point that the entire passage is building towards. And, it should be stated, not implied (this is generally true for SAT passages, at least).

When I say "building towards", that means you're looking for a clear line of reasoning. This causes this, which results in this final thing (thesis). Or, because of these several ideas, it is clear that ______ (thesis) is true. Something like that. You'll get better at identifying them as you go.

~See if you can find the thesis in this passage. It is, like everything in this passage, difficult. Write it down!

The thesis in this passage is the sentence in lines 30-34.

"As the ends of such a partnership cannot be obtained in many generations, it becomes a partnership not only between those who are living, but between those who are living, those who are dead, and those who are to be born."

The beginning adverb clause says "because that stuff I was talking about before can't happen in such a short time, the government must be the following things…" That is pretty clear thesis lingo.

And he goes on to say that the government must become a partnership among the dead, the living, and the yet-to-be-born. This further reinforces all his points about NOT changing the government. That would be disrespectful to the people who are dead, who can no longer give their opinions. So, we just can't change anything ever.

You and I can see the issues in such a statement, but it doesn't matter if you agree with Burke or not. (Thomas Paine will disagree with him in a second, don't worry.) You just have to know what he's saying.

Passage 2

Okay! It is finally time to get into the second passage of this pair.

Do this:

1. Read it. (Try not to cry too much.)
2. Find your main verb, subject, and direct object (if there is one) in each sentence.
3. Look for prepositional phrases, infinitives, and modifying clauses. Figure out what they modify. (If you want, you can draw arrows to show the modifying.)
4. Look for any places where Paine specifically responds to Burke's thesis.
5. Find Paine's thesis!
6. Write your SRS.

Every age and generation must be as free to act for itself, in all cases, as the ages and generations which preceded it. The vanity and presumption of governing beyond the grave, is the most ridiculous and insolent of all tyrannies.

Man has no property in man; neither has any generation a property in the generations which are to follow. The Parliament or the people of 1688, or of any other period, had no more right to dispose of the people of the present day, or to bind or to control them in any shape whatever, than the parliament or the people of the present day have to dispose of, bind, or control those who are to live a hundred or a thousand years hence.

Every generation is, and must be, competent to all the purposes which its occasions require. It is the living, and not the dead, that are to be accommodated. When man ceases to be, his power and his wants cease with him; and having no longer any participation in the concerns of this world, he has no longer any authority in directing who shall be its governors, or how its government shall be organized, or how administered. . . .

Those who have quitted the world, and those who are not yet arrived at it, are as remote from each other, as the utmost stretch of mortal imagination can conceive. What possible obligation, then, can exist between them; what rule or principle can be laid down, that two non-entities, the one out of existence, and the other not in, and who never can meet in this world, that the one should control the other to the end of time? . . .

The circumstances of the world are continually changing, and the opinions of men change also; and as government is for the living, and not for the dead, it is the living only that has any right in it. That which may be thought right and found convenient in one age, may be thought wrong and found inconvenient in another. In such cases, who is to decide, the living, or the dead?

Answers:

I'll show you the first two paragraphs!

Verbs will be made all caps, subjects will be underlined, direct objects will get {curly brackets}, phrases and clauses will get [brackets], infinitives will be noted in the bolded modifier notes.

(I'll leave out a few grammatical pieces that are more complicated to notate; for example, prepositions used with comparisons.)

Every age and generation MUST BE as free [to act] **(infinitive, modifying "free")** [for itself] **(modifies "act")**, [in all cases] (modifies "act"), as the ages and generations [which preceded it] **(adj clause, modifies "ages and generations")**. The vanity and presumption [of governing] **(modifies "vanity and presumption")** [beyond the grave] **(modifies "governing")**, IS the most ridiculous and insolent of all tyrannies **(predicate nominative in this sentence, not a direct object!)**.

Man HAS {no property} [in man] **(modifies "property")**; neither HAS any generation *(yes, I know it's backwards)* {a property} [in the generations] **(modifies "property")** [which are [to follow]] **(adj clause, modifies "generations", also infinitive inside the clause)**. The Parliament or the people [of 1688] **(modifies "people")**, or [of any other period] **(modifies "people")**, HAD {no more right} [to dispose] **(infinitive, modifies "right")** [of the people] **(modifies "dispose")** [of the present day] **(modifies "people")**, or [to bind] **(infinitive, modifies "dispose")** or [to control them] **(infinitive, modifies "dispose")** [in any shape whatever] **(modifies "control")**, than the parliament or the people [of the present day] **(modifies "the parliament or the people")** HAVE to dispose of, bind, or control those [who are to live a hundred or a thousand years hence] **(adj clause, modifies "those")**.

(I skipped over a bit of the end stuff there due to the complexity of comparisons and older English writing.)

Places where Paine responds to Burke:

LOL, trick question. It's just the whole entire passage. Literally every single sentence. If you were thinking that but didn't write down "the whole passage"…trust yourself more! If you wrote down "the whole passage", kudos.

Paine's Thesis: Again, a bit of a trick question. A LOT of his sentences have very clear, concise, and intense opinions in them. The first sentence is a pretty well summarized thesis. Also the first sentence of the second paragraph. Also the sentence in lines 58-63. Also the first sentence of the last paragraph.

Hopefully you didn't pick any of the sentences that end in a question mark. Theses do NOT end in a question mark. Theses are declarations, not curiosities. Even if a question is rhetorical, it's not likely going to be your thesis.

Finally, your SRS: I'd say something like this:

Paine be like, "The government is for the living. Also, I don't like Burke (lol)."

Make sure you're using the phrase "be like"! Don't make me have to lecture you! We gotta keep it funky!

So, Burke says government is for the dead, living, and not-yet-living, so don't go throwing a revolution! Paine says, "that's dumb."

Let's do the questions.

Question 32

In Passage 1, Burke indicates that a contract between a person and society differs from other contracts mainly in its

(A) brevity and prominence.
(B) complexity and rigidity.
(C) precision and usefulness.
(D) seriousness and permanence.

Pick an answer and write out an explanation!

The answer is D. The "lower" contracts (for coffee and pepper and stuff) were all about "objects of mere **occasional** interest…to be taken up for a little temporary interest, and to be dissolved by the fancy of the parties." Burke doesn't like that temporariness. He likes the government, which is permanent!

And then, obviously he thinks the government is more serious and stuff.

If you struggled with this one, it might have been the phrasing of the question. The "contract between a person and society" means government, pretty much. What holds a person accountable to and part of a society is the rules which govern that society and the governing body which enforces those rules. So, just like "the state" was another word for "the government", "society" also CAN be. Not always, though.

Question 33

As used in line 4, "state" most nearly refers to a

- **(A)** style of living.
- **(B)** position in life.
- **(C)** temporary condition.
- **(D)** political entity.

If you got this one wrong, after all the discussion we've done, you'll have to go invite all your friends over for a Laugh At You party…

Answer is D.

Question 34

As used in line 22, "low" most nearly means

(A) petty.
(B) weak.
(C) inadequate.
(D) depleted.

Answer is A. See how easy the questions are when you actually KNOW what the passage said? I know I won't be around to give you an hours long analysis of each passage on your real testing day, but with a few more practice tests (and other prep) you'll be able to do it for yourself!

Question 35

It can most reasonably be inferred from Passage 2 that Paine views historical precedents as

    (A) generally helpful to those who want to change society.
    (B) surprisingly difficult for many people to comprehend.
    (C) frequently responsible for human progress.
    (D) largely irrelevant to current political decisions.

Answer and explanation + evidence!

The answer is D.

Most students get this wrong because they don't actually know what historical precedents are. Write down what they are or look it up now!

Historical precedents are like milestones that will be referenced in the future. The Supreme Court is big on this. They're **constantly** talking about whatever historical precedent there is for making whatever ruling on a case. They also talk about how the ruling on this current case will set a precedent for the future, making it a really big deal…

"Historical precedents" would be set by people **in history**, aka dead people. Paine isn't super into dead people running the government and stuff. He wants living people to make new decisions. Meaning, whatever dead people did in history would be "irrelevant to current political decisions"!

Question 36

How would Paine most likely respond to Burke's statement in lines 30-34, Passage 1 ("As the...born")?

(A) He would assert that the notion of a partnership across generations is less plausible to people of his era than it was to people in the past.

(B) He would argue that there are no politically meaningful links between the dead, the living, and the unborn.

(C) He would question the possibility that significant changes to a political system could be accomplished within a single generation.

(D) He would point out that we cannot know what judgments the dead would make about contemporary issues.

Answer and evidence!!

B is exactly, word for word, Paine's whole point.

D is probably the distraction answer here. C is just Burke's opinion.

With D, it wouldn't matter if we knew what judgments the dead would make. Paine doesn't think their judgments should matter. This line of reasoning takes the logic to its end. It's a useful tactic, but logic is often harder for students these days, as it is not generally required learning in any schools. But, you can try to ask yourself, "Would it matter if this were true?" Or, in the reverse, "Would it matter if this were false?"

D is saying we cannot know, but would it really matter if we COULD know? If we knew exactly what Bob Smithington from the 1700s would have thought about our modern day issue, should we suddenly pay a lot of attention to that? No. So, D becomes irrelevant.

Question 37

Prior Question:

How would Paine most likely respond to Burke's statement in lines 30-34, Passage 1 ("As the...born")?

- **(A)** He would assert that the notion of a partnership across generations is less plausible to people of his era than it was to people in the past.
- **(B)** He would argue that there are no politically meaningful links between the dead, the living, and the unborn.
- **(C)** He would question the possibility that significant changes to a political system could be accomplished within a single generation.
- **(D)** He would point out that we cannot know what judgments the dead would make about contemporary issues.

Current Question:

Which choice provides the best evidence for the answer to the previous question?

- **(A)** Lines 41-43 ("Every . . . it")
- **(B)** Lines 43-45 ("The vanity . . . tyrannies")
- **(C)** Lines 56-58 ("It is . . . accommodated")
- **(D)** Lines 67-72 ("What . . . time")

This is a tougher one. Spend a bit of extra time.

Burke's statement: As the ends of such a partnership cannot be obtained in many generations, it becomes a partnership not only between those who are living, but between those who are living, those who are dead, and those who are to be born.

Paine's response (from the last question's answer): He would argue that there are no politically meaningful links between the dead, the living, and the unborn.

Here, we should break down what the answer choices are saying.

~Try to translate every quote to simple language.

A (lines 41-43) says that all people should be free to act for themselves.

B (lines 43-45) says governing "beyond the grave" (as in considering dead peoples' opinions) is vain, silly, and rude. If you didn't know the definition of "insolent"...Did you look it up!?! If not, **what are you doingggggg**? Do your vocab training; look up EVERY word you don't know. Get serious. Actually do this. Don't just read these words and think, "that's a good idea", and then ignore it. You need to improve your vocabulary. Now is the time to learn every word in every passage, question, and answer choice.

C (lines 56-58) says we should only think about the living.

D (lines 67-72) asks how we can expect there to be any connection or "obligation" between the dead and the unborn. It asks what rules or principles the now-dead could have made that should control the unborn. These are rhetorical questions.

The answer is D. D actually mentions those links/connections between the dead and the unborn and how Paine thinks such an idea is dumb. The other answer choices follow logically from this core idea, but they don't directly express the concept of the links.

Question 38

Which choice best describes how Burke would most likely have reacted to Paine's remarks in the final paragraph of Passage 2?

(A) With approval, because adapting to new events may enhance
existing partnerships.

(B) With resignation, because changing circumstances are an inevitable aspect of life.

(C) With skepticism, because Paine does not substantiate his claim
with examples of governments changed for the better.

(D) With disapproval, because changing conditions are insufficient
justification for changing the form of government.

Answer plus evidence!

So, hopefully you did not pick A. The whole point is that these guys disagree with each other in a very fundamental and complete way!

Answer is D. Paine's last paragraph discusses how opinions and needs always change, and the government needs to adapt to that. For evidence on Burke's response, hopefully you were looking at the end of his passage.

"The municipal corporations of that universal kingdom are not morally at liberty at their pleasure, and on their speculations of a contingent improvement, wholly to separate and tear asunder the bands of their subordinate community..."

And I'm sure you also looked up all of these words already!

So, this sentence is saying (simply) that local governments can't just tear apart their government because they think they can get some new benefits or improvement out of it. Again, this is Burke's opinion, not reality. In fact, America was largely founded on the importance of being able to change the government in response to changing conditions and needs.

Question 39

Which choice provides the best evidence for the answer to the previous question?

(A) Lines 1-4 ("To avoid . . . state")
(B) Lines 7-9 ("he should . . . solicitude")
(C) Lines 27-29 ("It is . . . perfection")
(D) Lines 34-38 ("The municipal . . . community")

This one we answered above: D.

Question 40

Which choice best states the relationship between the two passages?

- **(A)** Passage 2 challenges the primary argument of Passage 1.
- **(B)** Passage 2 advocates an alternative approach to a problem discussed in Passage 1.
- **(C)** Passage 2 provides further evidence to support an idea introduced in Passage 1.
- **(D)** Passage 2 exemplifies an attitude promoted in Passage 1.

Answer and reasoning/evidence!

These ones are hard because they're dense; every word is over 10 letters, making it annoying to read.

Disprove based on single words:

"Does passage 2 advocate for some kind of approach?" If yes, then,
"Does passage 1 discuss a problem?" If yes, then, "Is that approach an
alternative to that problem?"

"Is there an attitude in passage 1?" If yes, then, "Is passage 2 showing
an example of that attitude?"

You can do it for any answer.

The answer here is A. Many of the dual passages will be in direct
opposition, but sometimes the disagreements are smaller or nuanced
in some way, so you will usually see a question about the relationship
between the two passages on every test. **You can think about that
relationship when you first read the passages!**

Question 41

The main purpose of both passages is to

(A) suggest a way to resolve a particular political struggle.

(B) discuss the relationship between people and their government.

(C) evaluate the consequences of rapid political change.

(D) describe the duties that governments have to their citizens.

This is actually an ideal location for this question, because you will have spent the maximum amount of time possible reading and analyzing these two passages.

Small Tip: If you want to, you can skip all main purpose questions and answer them last for each passage. Just **be sure you don't mess up your scantron bubbles**. It happens, so don't just assume it won't happen to you.

For this one, I think your best bet is to ask yourself, "What would this look like?"

What would it look like if they were trying to highlight a "particular political struggle"? Well, there'd be mention of some specific struggle…obviously. A war, an uprising, a strike, a march… We don't have that here.

What about "rapid political change"? You would see a bigger discussion of the speed at which changes are happening. Something like, "This can't happen in so short a time." Or, "Decisions this important can't be resolved in only 4 years." Specific mentions of time.

Burke just hates all change and doesn't want it to happen at all, essentially. It's not about speed.

Remember, you're all naturally good at answering the question, "What would this look like if…?" Use that natural skill to your advantage!

Answer is B.

Some students pick D here because it initially sounds pretty similar to B. But, the passages aren't interested in how the government should be serving its people. If anything, Burke is more interested in how the people should be serving and taking care of their government!

Science Passage

This passage is adapted from Carolyn Gramling, *"Source of Mysterious Medieval Eruption Identified."* ©2013 by American Association for the Advancement of Science.

About 750 years ago, a powerful volcano erupted somewhere on Earth, kicking off a centuries-long cold snap known as the Little Ice Age. Identifying the volcano responsible has been tricky.

That a powerful volcano erupted somewhere in the world, sometime in the Middle Ages, is written in polar ice cores in the form of layers of sulfate deposits and tiny shards of volcanic glass. These cores suggest that the amount of sulfur the mystery volcano sent into the stratosphere put it firmly among the ranks of the strongest climate-perturbing eruptions of the current geological epoch, the Holocene, a period that stretches from 10,000 years ago to the present. A haze of stratospheric sulfur cools the climate by reflecting solar energy back into space.

In 2012, a team of scientists led by geochemist Gifford Miller strengthened the link between the mystery eruption and the onset of the Little Ice Age by using radiocarbon dating of dead plant material from beneath the ice caps on Baffin Island and Iceland, as well as ice and sediment core data, to determine that the cold summers and ice growth began abruptly between 1275 and 1300 C.E. (and became intensified between 1430 and 1455C.E.). Such a sudden onset pointed to a huge volcanic eruption injecting sulfur into the stratosphere and starting the cooling. Subsequent, unusually large and frequent eruptions of other volcanoes, as well as sea-ice/ocean feedbacks persisting long after the aerosols have been removed from the atmosphere, may have prolonged the cooling through the 1700s.

Volcanologist Franck Lavigne and colleagues now think they've identified the volcano in question: Indonesia's Samalas. One line of evidence, they note, is historical records. According to Babad Lombok, records of the island written on palm leaves in Old Javanese, Samalas erupted catastrophically before the end of the 13th century, devastating surrounding villages—including Lombok's capital at the time, Pamatan—with ash and fast-moving sweeps of hot rock and gas called pyroclastic flows.

The researchers then began to reconstruct the formation of the large, 800-meter-deep caldera [a basin-shaped volcanic crater] that now sits atop the volcano. They examined 130 outcrops on the flanks of the volcano, exposing sequences of pumice—ash hardened into rock— and other pyroclastic material. The volume of ash deposited, and the estimated height of the eruption plume (43 kilometers above sea level) put the eruption's magnitude at a minimum of 7 on the volcanic explosivity index (which has a scale of 1 to 8)—making it one of the largest known in the Holocene.

The team also performed radiocarbon analyses on carbonized tree trunks and branches buried within the pyroclastic deposits to confirm the date of the eruption; it could not, they concluded, have happened before 1257 C.E., and certainly happened in the 13th century.

It's not a total surprise that an Indonesian volcano might be the source of the eruption, Miller says. "An equatorial eruption is more consistent with the apparent climate impacts." And, he adds, with sulfate appearing in both polar ice caps—Arctic and Antarctic—there is "a strong consensus" that this also supports an equatorial source.

Another possible candidate—both in terms of timing and geographical location—is Ecuador's Quilotoa, estimated to have last erupted between 1147 and 1320 C.E. But when Lavigne's team examined shards of volcanic glass from this volcano, they found that they didn't match the chemical composition of the glass found in polar ice cores, whereas the Samalas glass is a much closer match. That, they suggest, further strengthens the case that Samalas was responsible for the medieval "year without summer" in 1258 C.E.

Estimated Temperature in Central England
1000 CE to 2000 CE

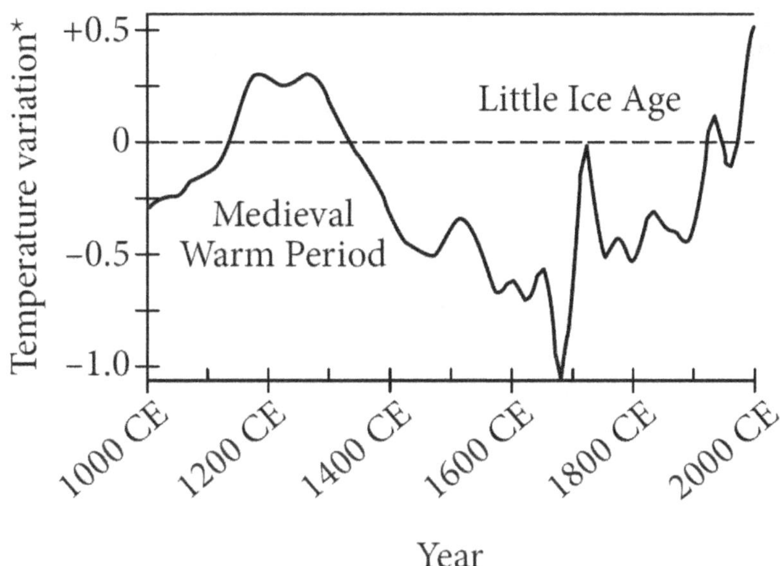

*Variation from the 1961-1990 average temperature, in °C, represented at 0.

Adapted from John P. Rafferty, "Little Ice Age." Originally published in 2011. ©2014 by Encyclopedia Britannica, Inc.

Do your SRS for the passage, and for the graph!

For the Passage: Some researchers be like, "What caused this mini Ice Age? I think it was this volcano."

For the Graph: How much the temperature differed from the late 1900s average.

This chart is really weird, so let's get through a few questions to be sure we know what information is being shown to us.

1. Around 1710, was the temperature generally above average, below, or at average?
2. From around 1130 to 1350, was the temperature generally 0.25 degrees?

   1. At average.
   2. No. The temperature was above the average by about that much.

Okay! Next a few questions about the passage.

   1. The researchers think that which volcano is responsible for the Little Ice Age?
   2. When did the Little Ice Age supposedly start?
   3. Give three reasons why the researchers think that the Samalas volcano caused the Little Ice Age.

1. The Samalas volcano.
2. About 750 years ago. Began abruptly between 1275 and 1300 CE.
3. ~There are layers of sulfate deposits and tiny shards of volcanic glass that are a closer match to Samalas.

   ~The volcano would have had to have been really intense, and Samalas is estimated to have been a 7 out of 8.

   ~Historical records say there was a catastrophic eruption before the end of the 13th century (same time as the Little Ice Age was starting).

   ~The researchers confirmed that the eruption of Samalas happened in the 13th century and could not have happened before 1257 (further supporting the timeline connection between the volcano and the ice age).

Any three of the above is great. If you found all four, even better!

Question 42

The main purpose of the passage is to

(A) describe periods in Earth's recent geologic history.

(B) explain the methods scientists use in radiocarbon analysis.

(C) describe evidence linking the volcano Samalas to the Little Ice Age.

(D) explain how volcanic glass forms during volcanic eruptions.

Hopefully you picked C! If not, ask yourself what each of the others should really have looked like.

For A, multiple periods listed out with date ranges and names. This passage is only concerned with the Little Ice Age.

For B, that would need to actually explain the radiocarbon process. Look up "radiocarbon dating" on Wikipedia. THAT is what a passage would look like for B to be true.

For D, same thing. It would be more like a Wikipedia article.

Question 43

Over the course of the passage, the focus shifts from

- **(A)** a criticism of a scientific model to a new theory.
- **(B)** a description of a recorded event to its likely cause.
- **(C)** the use of ice core samples to a new method of measuring sulfates.
- **(D)** the use of radiocarbon dating to an examination of volcanic glass.

Ask yourself what all of these would look like!

Answer **and evidence**.

Answer is B. You can also reference your Ridiculous Summary. This passage was about some scientists who wanted to know what caused the Little Ice Age and guessed that it was a volcano. Everything else is just supplementary (the radiocarbon dating, the ice core samples, the sulfate measuring, the volcanic glass…).

They start discussing this causal connection in paragraph 2. Most of the sentences in that paragraph would be good evidence for this one.

Question 44

Which choice provides the best evidence for the answer to the previous question?

    (A) Lines 17-25 ("In 2012 . . . 1455 C.E.")
    (B) Lines 43-46 ("The researchers . . . atop the volcano")
    (C) Lines 46-48 ("They examined . . . material")
    (D) Lines 55-60 ("The team . . . 13th century")

Answer is A.

Question 45

The author uses the phrase "is written in" (line 6) most likely to

(A) demonstrate the concept of the hands-on nature of the work done by scientists.

(B) highlight the fact that scientists often write about their discoveries.

(C) underscore the sense of importance that scientists have regarding their work.

(D) reinforce the idea that the evidence is there and can be interpreted by scientists.

Answer is D. What makes this one hard is the grammatical structure. This sentence contains a noun clause as the subject. If you struggled with this one, go master noun clauses!

Once you've done that, here's a tip: For noun clauses starting with "that", you can often replace it with "the fact that".

This: That a powerful volcano erupted somewhere in the world, sometime in the Middle Ages, is written in polar ice cores in the form of layers of sulfate deposits and tiny shards of volcanic glass.

Becomes This: The fact that a powerful volcano erupted somewhere in the world, sometime in the Middle Ages, is written in polar ice cores in the form of layers of sulfate deposits and tiny shards of volcanic glass.

That makes it a little easier to figure out what the sentence is trying to say!

Question 46

Where does the author indicate the medieval volcanic eruption most probably was located?

(A) Near the equator, in Indonesia
(B) In the Arctic region
(C) In the Antarctic region
(D) Near the equator, in Ecuador

Answer and direct textual evidence!!

Answer is A. This one is just surface-level reading. It's also weird that an equatorial volcano caused stuff to accumulate in polar ice caps, so some students think it can't be the equator. But, our world is very connected, especially environmentally! Also, the passage straight up says it in the most obvious way.

The 7th paragraph (next to last) contains the evidence for this question.

Question 47

Which choice provides the best evidence for the answer to the previous question?

- **(A)** Lines 1-3 ("About 750 . . . Ice Age")
- **(B)** Lines 26-28 ("Such a . . . the cooling")
- **(C)** Lines 49-54 ("The volume . . . the Holocene")
- **(D)** Lines 61-64 ("It's not . . . climate impacts")

Answer is D.

Question 48

As used in line 68, the phrase "Another possible candidate" implies that

    (A) powerful volcanic eruptions occur frequently.

    (B) the effects of volcanic eruptions can last for centuries.

    (C) scientists know of other volcanoes that erupted during the Middle Ages.

    (D) other volcanoes have calderas that are very large.

Answer is C. This is a good one for understanding what, exactly, something can prove or imply.

A lot of students (and people in general) take things too far. For example, just because there is another candidate, doesn't mean that there are frequent volcanic eruptions. It might be JUST those two, or maybe 3 or 5, and that wouldn't necessarily mean "frequent".

In colloquial English, we tend to exaggerate a lot (at least in America, and especially for younger people). But, this is exactly the time to not exaggerate at all, and to be very literal.

The other possible candidate MIGHT also have a large caldera, but you don't know that for sure. It might have a mid-sized caldera! Who knows? The point is, take things very much at face value.

Question 49

As used in line 68, the phrase "Another possible candidate" implies that

- **(A)** powerful volcanic eruptions occur frequently.
- **(B)** the effects of volcanic eruptions can last for centuries.
- **(C)** scientists know of other volcanoes that erupted during the Middle Ages.
- **(D)** other volcanoes have calderas that are very large.

Which choice best supports the claim that Quilotoa was not responsible for the Little Ice Age?

- **(A)** Lines 3-4 ("Identifying . . . tricky")
- **(B)** Lines 26-28 ("Such a . . . cooling")
- **(C)** Lines 43-46 ("The researchers . . . atop the volcano")
- **(D)** Lines 71-75 ("But . . . closer match")

Why yes, I did attempt to trick you again! You're welcome.

Did you fall for the SAT's trick (and mine)? If not, good. If you're super confused reading this right now…go back and actually read the current question!

The SAT will do this at least once on your test. Don't just assume that it's asking for evidence to the previous question!

This one should be pretty easy because Quilotoa is ONLY discussed in the last paragraph, and the only quote from that paragraph is answer choice D. And also that quote is good evidence for why they think it's not Quilotoa.

Question 50

Estimated Temperature in Central England
1000 CE to 2000 CE

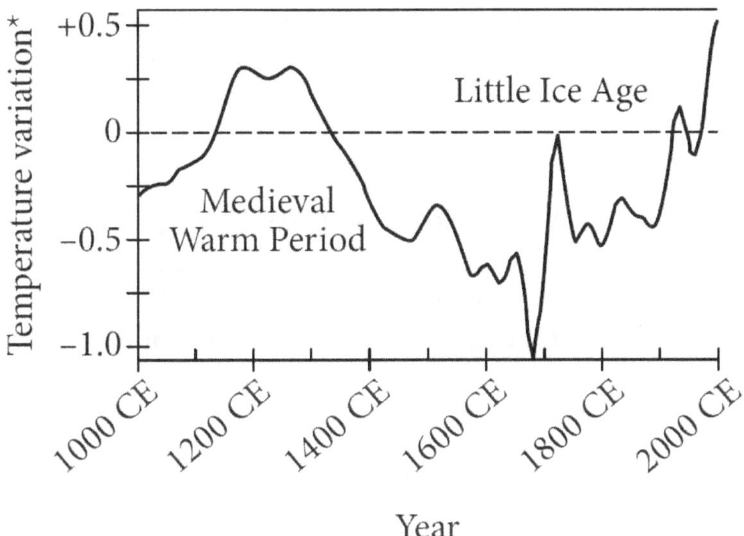

*Variation from the 1961-1990 average temperature, in °C, represented at 0.

Adapted from John P. Rafferty, "Little Ice Age." Originally published in 2011.
©2014 by Encyclopedia Britannica, Inc.

According to the data in the figure, the greatest below-average temperature variation occurred around what year?

(A) 1200 CE
(B) 1375 CE
(C) 1675 CE
(D) 1750 CE

I have known several very bright students to get this one wrong. It was always a matter of rounding poorly and being imprecise.

My recommendation: On graphs, there are tick marks. Generally, you can easily, visually divide the space between tick marks into 4 equal bits (maybe 5). Do that, and then get as close to one of those fourths lines as you can. Don't just round up to the next big line, because that will likely throw you off!

Answer is C.

Remember, this graph is looking at deviation from the average. So, the greatest below-average variation point would be wherever the graph has the biggest negative point ("greatest negative" means the most negative point). It's actually touching the bottom of the graph, so it should be easy to identify.

Question 51

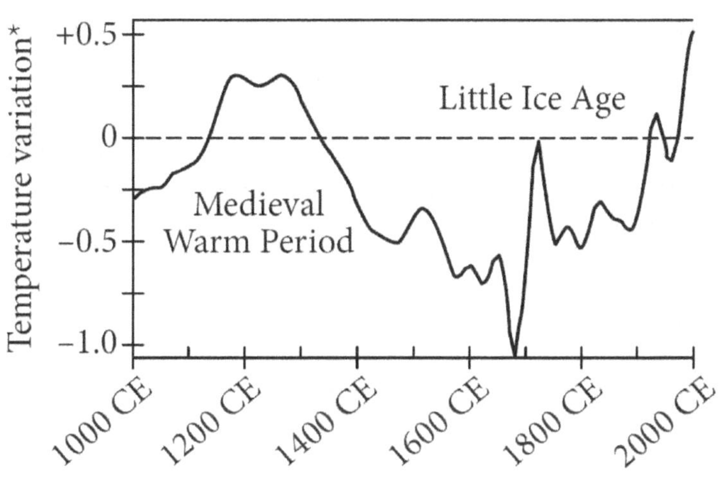

*Variation from the 1961-1990 average temperature, in °C, represented at 0.

Adapted from John P. Rafferty, "Little Ice Age." Originally published in 2011. ©2014 by Encyclopedia Britannica, Inc.

The passage and the figure are in agreement that the onset of the Little Ice Age began

- **(A)** around 1150 CE.
- **(B)** just before 1300 CE.
- **(C)** just before 1500 CE.
- **(D)** around 1650 CE.

Answer + find the quote from the passage that says when the Little Ice Age began!

Answer is B. The quote is in lines 23-24: "…the cold summers and ice growth

began abruptly between 1275 and 1300 C.E…"

Personally, I think the graph is a little unhelpful here. Sure, the temperature is starting to decrease around 1275, but it's also still higher than the average overall. If we decide that the start of the decrease = the start of the Ice Age, then that's fine. But, it doesn't exactly say that anywhere. Someone could just as easily say that the Ice Age didn't start until we dropped past a certain average point (or something).

Regardless, when in doubt, the passage should have good evidence for you, and it does!

Question 52

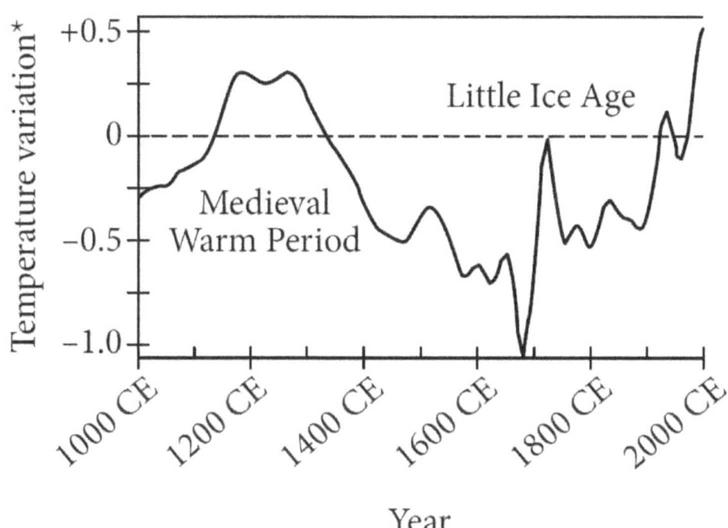

*Variation from the 1961-1990 average temperature, in °C, represented at 0.

Adapted from John P. Rafferty, "Little Ice Age." Originally published in 2011. ©2014 by Encyclopedia Britannica, Inc.

What statement is best supported by the data presented in the figure?

(A) The greatest cooling during the Little Ice Age occurred hundreds of years after the temperature peaks of the Medieval Warm Period.

(B) The sharp decline in temperature supports the hypothesis of an equatorial volcanic eruption in the Middle Ages.

(C) Pyroclastic flows from volcanic eruptions continued for hundreds of years after the eruptions had ended.

(D) Radiocarbon analysis is the best tool scientists have to determine the temperature variations after volcanic eruptions.

Keep in mind what a graph can and cannot tell you. This graph CAN tell you the date and the temperature variation. It cannot tell you how long volcanoes lasted or which scientific tool is best or whether or not equatorial volcanoes erupted. That would need support from the passage, other data, etc.

Answer is A. You can see the gap of hundreds of years clearly in the graph.

Reading Selected Passages (and Advanced Homework)

Instructions

At this point, you will diversify your work.

Walk through the next several selected passages from real SAT tests with me. I'll tell you where every passage comes from, so you can take the full tests (or just the reading sections, if you prefer) before looking over my analysis, admonitions, and convivial mockery of your bad habits!

I'll only review a few of the harder questions for each passage to help keep this a true crash course.

You should follow along and take the College Board official tests in the order I have them listed. I'll indicate how many questions you should be getting correct with each successive test!

A note on vocab: In these passages, I won't be going over the words in context questions. If you're still having trouble with that, do more Vocab Synapse. Make more flashcards for any words in any passages that you don't know. Make flashcards for any words in any question or answer choice that you don't know. Look up words online to find not only their denotation (definition) but also their connotations (deeper meaning, common usage, etc.).

A note on evidence questions: I will also not be including the evidence questions in these selected passages. A great many students struggle with the evidence questions, so you might question my judgement here. I'll explain: You MUST practice finding evidence for every question, not just the questions that ask for it. So, you will be reminded to find your evidence with every question, and I will indicate the best evidence to support the correct answer for every question. In this way, you'll get 5 times as much practice with this skill!

Now on to the next big thing.

You should ALSO start doing harder passages! I've compiled MCAT passages on our website here: www.VohraMethod.com/mcat-passages. They're broken down by days, but you don't have to do them on back-to-back days. Just work through them as quickly as you can, alongside the following SAT work.

Each passage has 4-6 questions, so nothing crazy. But, they are much more challenging in terms of language density and difficulty of finding the right evidence.

As you go through the passages, be sure to do your SRS! Working through the questions, actually write down the sentence that you think shows the evidence for your answer choice. DON'T skip this step like a Lazy McLazerton. The number one skill you need for every single passage type on the SAT is the ability to find the RIGHT evidence. That's what you need to practice.

All the other questions about Tone or Implications or Chart+Passage Synthesis…They all rely on your ability to find the right supporting evidence in the passage.

So, write out your selected evidence. If anything doesn't make sense, come meet with me or find another tutor. You need to work towards 100% comprehension, not your school's usual half-butt, 93-percent-is-still-an-A style of nonsense. To get a near perfect score on the SAT, you need at minimum 99% accuracy. To get a perfect score you need…100% accuracy! (obv)

Okay! **Two big tasks: Selected Passages below and MCAT CARS passages online.** Proceed!

Akira (Test 1)

Along with this passage, complete 3 MCAT passages.

You can take the full test 1 before reviewing these selected questions. For every question you get wrong on test 1, physically write down a clear explanation of why the answer you picked was wrong. Then, take another guess for the correct answer. (This requires that you always write your answers on a separate sheet and grade them simply by marking them right or wrong. That way you will know if the question is wrong, but you won't know the correct answer.)

If you get more than 10 questions wrong on the reading section of test 1, you should come see me: CSnyder@VohraMethod.com. If you get fewer than 10 wrong, then you're on track. Keep working!

Experiment: For this test, really lean into your SRS. You don't have to take this test timed.

Write your SRS on paper. Then, answer as many questions as you can with ONLY that. Don't look back at the passage. Don't do any of the evidence questions, and ignore the words in context ones, of course. Just see how many questions you can get right using the SRS alone. Try this for every type of passage.

If your instincts are way off the mark, come see me. If your Simple Ridiculous Summaries aren't helping you at all, come see me.

You'll notice that your SRS won't help you for **every** question, but it will for quite a lot of them. As you go along, you will probably try to revert back to your old ways and not do the SRS at all. You should obviously not do that, because your old ways clearly did not work.

For now, write your SRS summary by hand on paper. Over time, you might start to just put a few key words. But, don't get obsessed with "saving time" just yet. We have plenty of other tests for that.

Read this passage and do your ridiculous summary. Then, we'll see if you understood the crux of this passage with a couple of questions!

This passage is from Lydia Minatoya, *The Strangeness of Beauty*. ©1999 by Lydia Minatoya. The setting is Japan in 1920. Chie and her daughter Naomi are members of the House of Fuji, a noble family.

Akira came directly, breaking all tradition. Was that it? Had he followed form – had he asked his mother to speak to his father to approach a go-between—would Chie have been more receptive?

He came on a winter's eve. He pounded on the door while a cold rain beat on the shuttered veranda, so at first Chie thought him only the wind. The maid knew better. Chie heard her soft scuttling footsteps, the creak of the door. Then the maid brought a calling card to the drawing room, for Chie.

Chie was reluctant to go to her guest; perhaps she was feeling too cozy. She and Naomi were reading at a low table set atop a charcoal brazier. A thick quilt spread over the sides of the table so their legs were tucked inside with the heat.

"Who is it at this hour, in this weather?" Chie questioned as she picked the name card off the maid's lacquer tray.

"Shinoda, Akira. Kobe Dental College," she read.

Naomi recognized the name. Chie heard a soft intake of air.

"I think you should go," said Naomi.

Akira was waiting in the entry. He was in his early twenties, slim and serious, wearing the black military-style uniform of a student. As he bowed—his hands hanging straight down, a black cap in one, a yellow oil-paper umbrella in the other—Chie glanced beyond him. In the glistening surface of the courtyard's rain-drenched paving stones, she saw his reflection like a dark double.

"Madame," said Akira, "forgive my disruption, but I come with a matter of urgency."

His voice was soft, refined. He straightened and stole a deferential peek at her face.

In the dim light his eyes shone with sincerity. Chie felt herself starting to like him.

"Come inside, get out of this nasty night. Surely your business can wait for a moment or two."

"I don't want to trouble you. Normally I would approach you more properly, but I've received word of a position. I've an opportunity to go to America, as dentist for Seattle's Japanese community."

"Congratulations," Chie said with amusement. "That is an opportunity, I'm sure. But how am I involved?"

Even noting Naomi's breathless reaction to the name card, Chie had no idea. Akira's message, delivered like a formal speech, filled her with maternal amusement. You know how children speak so earnestly, so hurriedly, so endearingly about things that have no importance in an adult's mind? That's how she viewed him, as a child.

It was how she viewed Naomi. Even though Naomi was eighteen and training endlessly in the arts needed to make a good marriage, Chie had made no effort to find her a husband.

Akira blushed.

"Depending on your response, I may stay in Japan. I've come to ask for Naomi's hand."

Suddenly Chie felt the dampness of the night. "Does Naomi know anything of your... ambitions?"

"We have an understanding. Please don't judge my candidacy by the unseemliness of this proposal. I ask directly because the use of a go-between takes much time. Either method comes down to the same thing: a matter of parental approval. If you give your consent, I become Naomi's yoshi.* We'll live in the House of Fuji. Without your consent, I must go to America, to secure a new home for my bride."

Eager to make his point, he'd been looking her full in the face. Abruptly, his voice turned gentle. "I see I've startled you. My humble apologies. I'll take no more of your evening. My address is on my card. If you don't wish to contact me, I'll reapproach you in two weeks' time. Until then, good night."

He bowed and left. Taking her ease, with effortless grace, like a cat making off with a fish.

"Mother?" Chie heard Naomi's low voice and turned from the door. "He has asked you?"

The sight of Naomi's clear eyes, her dark brows gave Chie strength. Maybe his hopes were preposterous.

"Where did you meet such a fellow? Imagine! He thinks he can marry the Fuji heir and take her to America all in the snap of his fingers!"

Chie waited for Naomi's ripe laughter.

Naomi was silent. She stood a full half minute looking straight into Chie's eyes. Finally, she spoke.

"I met him at my literary meeting."

Naomi turned to go back into the house, then stopped.

"Mother." "Yes?"

"I mean to have him."

* a man who marries a woman of higher status and takes her family's name

Post-Passage Questions

1. Write your SRS!

   (This passage actually has a lot of actions in it. That's less common for a fiction passage, but most of it is just one big conversation. So, we can set aside our focus on actions here.)

2. Okay! Now figure this out: What is a "go-between"?

1. SRS: Basically, a dude shows up to this girl's parent's house and be like, "I wanna marry your daughter."

I actually laugh so much at this passage. It reminds me of the song Rude by MAGIC!. The artist is asking for a father's permission to marry his daughter (the dad says no), and then the artists exclaims, "Why you gotta be so rude? I'm gonna marry her anyways."

Here, Akira says, "If you give your consent, I become Naomi's yoshi. We'll live in the House of Fuji. Without your consent, I must go to America, to secure a new home for my bride." So… if the mom doesn't consent, then he's just going to take Naomi with him to America.

It's not exactly the same, but you can get a humorous feel for the passage, anyways. Remember, keep it fun!

2. Now, on to the "go-between". Sometimes on SAT tests you will have to figure a few things out. Context clues, logic, etc. This is nothing new.

You should make yourself aware of various cultures around the world. The SAT likes to pull passages from non-American cultures and also from older time periods. Older time periods will have different cultural norms, beliefs, etc.

You don't need to be an expert on all cultures throughout all of time. But, you should generally know that there were nomadic cultures and big city cultures. There were rigid societies and more casual ones. There were strict gender roles. There were differing ideas about politeness and manners. There were (and are) big differences between Eastern and Western cultures. There is a huge difference between European and American culture.

Just knowing that those sentences above are true is enough to get you started. After that, you just ask yourself, "What kind of culture is there in this passage?"

In this Akira passage, the culture is more formal, rules-based. It probably has some pretty specific gender roles and rules about social etiquette. So, when it says:

Had he followed form – had he asked his mother to speak to his father to approach a go-between—would Chie have been more receptive?

The word "form" suggests that this is the usual set of rules that he maybe should be following. Next, we can get into grammar.

The dashes used here indicate a clear modifier (or redefinition) of the word "form". So, the proper form would have been to ask his mother to speak to his father to approach this "go-between". That sort of idea pretty much screams "**matchmaker**".

Matchmakers were really common in many cultures throughout much of history. It's the kind of thing you should be generally aware of.

Question 1

Which choice best describes what happens in the passage?

- **(A)** One character argues with another character who intrudes on her home.
- **(B)** One character receives a surprising request from another character.
- **(C)** One character reminisces about choices she has made over the years.
- **(D)** One character criticizes another character for pursuing an unexpected course of action.

Find your evidence!

Two trick wrong answers here.

A is wrong because Akira isn't **intruding**. Intruding is a much bigger thing that carries legal ramifications. He just shows up unexpectedly. Some students pick this because they think of it as like, "he intruded on their nice evening". That is a way that "intrude" can be used, but when it's used that way, it's always followed by "on".

The other one students sometimes pick is D. Again, just reading too much into it. We get the feeling that Chie is surprised and maybe she even slightly disapproves of **the way** he's doing this. But, she doesn't actually criticize him at any point in the passage. It says she thinks of him as a "child", but that's not a criticism (it's just a feeling). Akira also mentions the "unseemliness" of his proposal (this being because he didn't use a "go-between" and all that). But Chie doesn't criticize him openly for that.

Correct answer is B.

Best Evidence: Showing that Chie was surprised: "Even noting Naomi's breathless reaction to the name card, Chie had no idea."

Showing that Chie received a request: "I've come to ask for Naomi's hand."

Question 2

Which choice best describes the developmental pattern of the passage?

(A) A careful analysis of a traditional practice

(B) A detailed depiction of a meaningful encounter

(C) A definitive response to a series of questions

(D) A cheerful recounting of an amusing anecdote

The trick answer here is A. The traditional practice of using a go-between is a huge crux of this passage, but it's not being carefully analyzed. In fact, you have to figure out what a go-between even is all on your own. If it were an analysis, then it would at least tell you what a go-between is…

Correct answer is B.

Question 4

Which reaction does Akira most fear from Chie?

    (A) She will consider his proposal inappropriate.
    (B) She will mistake his earnestness for immaturity.
    (C) She will consider his unscheduled visit an imposition.
    (D) She will underestimate the sincerity of his emotions.

Find your evidence!

All of the wrong answers are tricky here. B is wrong, but students often pick it because Chie mentions viewing Akira like a child. C is wrong, but students often pick it because Akira does, in fact, visit unexpectedly. And D is wrong; it usually gets picked because the passage happens to mention that Akira's "eyes shone with sincerity" and, I think, because students get the idea that Akira and Naomi haven't known each other for very long and couldn't possibly love each other enough to be married.

All of this is reading too much into the passage and/or doing those terrible Mental Gymnastics. This question is asking what **Akira** is afraid of. The question is NOT asking you what happens to be true in Chie's mind. So, even though Chie does mention viewing Akira as a child, Akira's biggest fear can be (and is) something completely other than being perceived as immature.

From the very start of the passage, we can see that Akira is worried about how this proposal for marriage is going to go. He questions his decision not to follow proper form and use a matchmaker.

Again, it is quite possibly true that Chie considers this visit to be an imposition. The passage tells us that she is warm by their brazier, and she doesn't want to get up to go to the door. Still though, that doesn't mean that is what **Akira** is most afraid of.

D is the weakest trick answer here. You can ask yourself what D would really look like in the passage. You would have Akira worriedly wondering if Chie would believe that he means it, that he's serious. Maybe Akira would verbally say, "Please don't view this visit as a lack of sincerity."

Instead, Akira says, "Please don't judge my candidacy by the **unseemliness of this proposal**." That's nearly word for word what answer choice A says.

Best Evidence: "Please don't judge my candidacy by the unseemliness of this proposal."

Question 9

Why does Akira say his meeting with Chie is "a matter of urgency?"

    (A) He fears that his own parents will disapprove of Naomi.

    (B) He worries that Naomi will reject him and marry someone else.

    (C) He has been offered an attractive job in another country.

    (D) He knows that Chie is unaware of his feelings for Naomi.

Find your evidence!

Again here, just because D is true, doesn't make it the correct answer. Imagine I ask you what your name is and you tell me, "D.C. is the capital of America." That didn't answer my question. Truth isn't the point here. Answering the actual question being asked is the point!

Correct answer is C.

Best Evidence: "Normally I would approach you more properly but I've received word of a position. I've an opportunity to go to America, as dentist for Seattle's Japanese community."

The first sentence explains that he is rushing things a bit. The second sentence explains why.

Nawabdin (Test 6)

Along with this passage, complete 3 MCAT passages.

You can take the full test 6 before reviewing these selected questions. I have included one other passage from test 6. It is the historical dual passage one. At the end of this section.

For every question you get wrong on test 6, physically write down a clear explanation of why the answer you picked was wrong. Then, take another guess for the correct answer. (This requires that you always write your answers on a separate sheet and grade them simply by marking them right or wrong. That way you will know if the question is wrong, but you won't know the correct answer.)

If you get more than 8 questions wrong on the reading section of test 6, you should come see me: CSnyder@VohraMethod.com. If you get fewer than 8 wrong, then you're on track. Keep working!

Experiment: On this test, you'll practice your SAT intuition. You do not have to take this test time.

SAT intuition is that magical thing that students are always referring to called "test taking ability" or something similar. It's not magic; it turns out. It's just logic. Here's how you practice:

For all NON-fiction passages, DO NOT read the passage. You can read **just** the passage intro information to know the general topic. Then, read through the questions (skip the words in context ones and the evidence ones) and look for any answer choices that are either highly likely or highly unlikely without ever having read the passage.

You'll find that there are plenty of answer choices that are just almost certainly not the answer, unless the passage takes some big and very obvious and unexpected turn... You'll find that there are some answer choices that are very probably right just given what you know about the context of the discussion surrounding women throughout history, or the way that the scientific method works (hypothesis, test, conclusion...for the most part).

And you'll find that sometimes, a full THREE answer choices are very, very unlikely, and ONE seems quite likely. Meaning, sometimes you can get the answer from logic and general world knowledge alone, without having read the passage at all.

On the real test, you'll read the passage and then answer the questions. But, you will have practiced this skill of looking plainly at what is likely or unlikely based on general knowledge, so you won't get tricked by answer choices that are wildly weird but just happen to contain a few memorable words from the passage.

Sometimes, you'll end up with just two that are unlikely, and two answer choices that are possible candidates. This can help you to see the difference between a logical answer and...**a logical answer that is actually supported by the passage.** That's a critical differentiation!

Again, try this for the science and history passages, not for the fiction. Fiction is all made up, so you can't really "logic" your way through it.

Read this passage and do your ridiculous summary. Then, we'll see if you understood the crux of this passage with a couple of questions!

This passage is adapted from Daniyal Mueenuddin, *"Nawabdin Electrician."* ©2009 by Daniyal Mueenuddin.

Another man might have thrown up his hands—but not Nawabdin. His twelve daughters acted as a spur to his genius, and he looked with satisfaction in the mirror each morning at the face of a warrior going out to do battle. Nawab of course knew that he must proliferate his sources of revenue—the salary he received from K. K. Harouni for tending the tube wells would not even begin to suffice. He set up a little one-room flour mill, run off a condemned electric motor—condemned by him. He tried his hand at fish-farming in a little pond at the edge of his master's fields. He bought broken radios, fixed them, and resold them. He did not demur even when asked to fix watches, though that enterprise did spectacularly badly, and in fact earned him more kicks than kudos, for no watch he took apart ever kept time again.

K. K. Harouni rarely went to his farms, but lived mostly in Lahore. Whenever the old man visited, Nawab would place himself night and day at the door leading from the servants' sitting area into the walled grove of ancient banyan trees where the old farmhouse stood. Grizzled, his peculiar aviator glasses bent and smudged, Nawab tended the household machinery, the air conditioners, water heaters, refrigerators, and water pumps, like an engineer tending the boilers on a foundering steamer in an Atlantic gale. By his superhuman efforts he almost managed to maintain K. K. Harouni in the same mechanical cocoon, cooled and bathed and lighted and fed, that the landowner enjoyed in Lahore.

Harouni of course became familiar with this ubiquitous man, who not only accompanied him on his tours of inspection, but morning and night could be found standing on the master bed rewiring the light fixture or in the bathroom poking at the water heater. Finally, one evening at teatime, gauging the psychological moment, Nawab asked if he might say a word. The landowner, who was cheerfully filing his nails in front of a crackling rosewood fire, told him to go ahead.

"Sir, as you know, your lands stretch from here to the Indus, and on these lands are fully seventeen tube wells, and to tend these seventeen tube wells there is but one man, me, your servant. In your service I have earned these gray hairs"—here he bowed his head to show the gray—"and now I cannot fulfill my duties as I should. Enough, sir, enough. I beg you, forgive me my weakness. Better a darkened house and proud hunger within than disgrace in the light of day. Release me, I ask you, I beg you."

The old man, well accustomed to these sorts of speeches, though not usually this florid, filed away at his nails and waited for the breeze to stop.

"What's the matter, Nawabdin?"

"Matter, sir? O what could be the matter in your service. I've eaten your salt for all my years. But sir, on the bicycle now, with my old legs, and with the many injuries I've received when heavy machinery fell on me—I cannot any longer bicycle about like a bridegroom from farm to farm, as I could when I first had the good fortune to enter your employment. I beg you, sir, let me go."

"And what's the solution?" asked Harouni, seeing that they had come to the crux. He didn't particularly care one way or the other, except that it touched on his comfort—a matter of great interest to him.

"Well, sir, if I had a motorcycle, then I could somehow limp along, at least until I train up some younger man."

The crops that year had been good, Harouni felt expansive in front of the fire, and so, much to the disgust of the farm managers, Nawab received a brand-new motorcycle, a Honda 70. He even managed to extract an allowance for gasoline.

The motorcycle increased his status, gave him weight, so that people began calling him "Uncle," and asking his opinion on world affairs, about which he knew absolutely nothing. He could now range further, doing a much wider business. Best of all, now he could spend every night with his wife, who had begged to live not on the farm but near her family in Firoza, where also they could educate at least the two eldest daughters. A long straight road ran from the canal headworks near Firoza all the way to the Indus, through the heart of the K. K. Harouni lands. Nawab would fly down this road on his new machine, with bags and cloths hanging from every knob and brace, so that the bike, when he hit a bump, seemed to be flapping numerous small vestigial wings; and with his grinning face, as he rolled up to whichever tube well needed servicing, with his ears almost blown off, he shone with the speed of his arrival.

Post-Passage Questions

1. Do your SRS.

    (Again, here, the action is primarily one big conversation. There are some actions described in the beginning, but they happened in the past. Then we have the action of riding around on the motorcycle. That will have a question with it! The majority of the questions, though, are going to relate to the conversation.)

2. Did Nawabdin really want to quit working?

Answers:

1. Something like: This dude has a plan to get a motorcycle and
    he succeeds.

    Nothing else in the passage is central to the point! Not his
    daughters or what work he does or whatever. Remember to
    keep these very simple and short.

2. No, he did not!

How do we know?

First, he starts out his speech this way:

"Finally, one evening at teatime, **gauging the psychological moment**, Nawab asked if he might say a word."

Then, he drones on and on about how much land Harouni has (compliments) and how gray Nawab's own hair is (laying on the guilt).

Then, we see this about Harouni:

"The old man, **well accustomed to these sorts of speeches**, though not usually this florid, filed away at his nails and waited for the breeze to stop."

What sorts of speeches? (You should be asking yourself…)

Then, Nawab does some more complimenting of Harouni and begs (again) to be allowed to quit. To which Harouni replies, " 'What is the solution?'…**seeing that they had come to the crux**." Meaning, Harouni isn't taking this speech all that seriously.

Then, instead of saying that the solution is, as he has asked twice now, to be allowed to quit and retire…Nawab says that **the solution is a motorbike**.

So, there you have it. It was all a ploy to get a motorcycle from his employer. You can ask yourself what it would have looked like if Nawab had truly wanted to retire/quit. It would have been a short, boring passage about a dude who goes to his employer and directly asks if he can retire, without all these theatrics.

Question 1

The main purpose of the first paragraph is to

(A) characterize Nawab as a loving father.
(B) outline the schedule of a typical day in Nawab's life.
(C) describe Nawab's various moneymaking ventures.
(D) contrast Nawab's and Harouni's lifestyles.

Find your evidence within the first paragraph!

A lot of students pick A here. But, ask yourself what it would really look like if the passage were trying to show a loving father. Would it mention the daughters briefly, in half a sentence, and then transition back to talking about Nawab looking at himself in the mirror with satisfaction? That sounds more narcissistic than externally loving.

Also, if you're ever not sure for main purpose, I recommend literally just counting sentences (or paragraphs). If a question asks for the main idea of a whole passage and you're stuck between two answer choices, count how many paragraphs relate to each of those two answer choices. It's almost never equal. Usually, one topic is the clear winner, showing up in over half of the paragraphs (or at least all of the biggest paragraphs).

Inside one paragraph, count the sentences in the same way. You're literally looking to see how much real estate an idea takes up. More real estate on the page equals more likely to be the main idea.

Correct answer is C.

Best Evidence: Starting at line 5, the paragraph details Nawab's attempts at a "flour mill", "fish-farming", fixing radios, and fixing watches. It's also suggested that he broke an electric motor while trying to fix it. That's a lot of ventures!

Question 5

In the context of the conservation between Nawab and Harouni,
Nawab's comments in lines 43-52 mainly serve to

(A) Flatter Harouni by mentioning how vast his lands are
(B) Boast to Harouni about how competent and reliable Nawab is
(C) Emphasize Nawab's diligence and loyalty to Harouni
(D) Notify Harouni that Nawab intends to quit his job tending the
tube wells

Find your evidence!

Everyone always picks D because no one realizes that what a person SAYS isn't always what that person MEANS.

However, I would like to note that you guys ALL know that!!! You all have experienced someone who directly lied to you, or who just hid or obscured the truth. You've all talked to a person who said he/she was "fine", when in reality that was not true.

So, don't be silly. People SAY all kinds of things.

We already have the evidence for why D is wrong. That was in the post-passage question. So, not it's down to B and C. Students do sometimes pick B, because the two seem quite similar. But, remember that Nawab's plan is to essentially butter up his employer so he can get a motorcycle. Is NOW the time to be **boasting** about how great you are?

No.

So, I would ditch B based on the word "boast".

And C makes sense because when Harouni is reminded of how diligent and loyal Nawab is, he might be tempted to reward that loyalty… with a motorcycle!

Question 7

It can be reasonably inferred from the passage that Harouni provides Nawab with a motorcycle mainly because

- **(A)** Harouni appreciates that Nawab has to work hard to support his family
- **(B)** Harouni sees benefit to himself from giving Nawab a motorcycle
- **(C)** Nawab's speech is the most eloquent that Harouni has ever heard
- **(D)** Nawab threatens to quit if Harouni doesn't agree to give him a motorcycle

Find your evidence!

D is a distracting answer here. The problem with D is that Nawab isn't "threatening" Harouni. Nawab is being manipulative, sure. But, direct threats wouldn't help him get a motorcycle. Nawab has to be clever.

Correct answer is B.

Best Evidence: "He didn't particularly care one way or the other, except that it touched on his comfort—a matter of great interest to him."

Question 9

The passage states that the farm managers react to Nawab receiving a motorcycle with

(A) Disgust
(B) Happiness
(C) Envy
(D) Indifference

Find your evidence!

I include this one because it's another instance of two characters being introduced really close together, creating unnecessary confusion.

The farm managers show disgust. The "people" are happy with him, maybe even envious. It increases his status. Who are these "people"? Who cares. The question isn't asking about them. It's just a bunch of irrelevant people introduced at once, and the ones we want to know about are the farm managers.

Answer is A.

Best Evidence: "…much to the **disgust** of the farm managers, Nawab received a brand-new motorcycle, a Honda 70."

Old Widow Lau (Test 9)

Along with this passage, complete 3 MCAT passages.

You can take the full test 9 before reviewing these selected questions.

For every question you get wrong on test 9, physically write down a clear explanation of why the answer you picked was wrong. Then, take another guess for the correct answer. (This requires that you always write your answers on a separate sheet and grade them simply by marking them right or wrong. That way you will know if the question is wrong, but you won't know the correct answer.)

If you get more than 6 questions wrong on the reading section of test 9, you should come see me: CSnyder@VohraMethod.com. If you get fewer than 6 wrong, then you're on track. Keep working!

For this test (and all following), do it timed. *(If you have significant timing issues, like running out of time on the whole last passage, or not being able to answer 2 or more questions at the end, come see me right away.)*

I highly encourage you to continue experimenting with SAT Intuition by trying to answer questions without reading the passages at all. You can do this untimed, and then go back and take the test timed. Or, you can try to do it all within the alloted time for the test. Again, you're experimenting. You're not trying to be perfect yet. You're just trying to get better.

Some students like to try reading over the questions first, then reading the passage. The idea is that you have a better idea of what to focus on and look for. I think this works for some and doesn't work for others. The way you'll know is that you'll try both. I just read the passage first and remember it all. I'm an avid reader, and I don't have trouble with that method.

Just experiment and go for it!

Read this passage and do your ridiculous summary. Then, we'll see if you understood the crux of this passage with a couple of questions!

This passage is adapted from Amy Tan, *The Bonesetter's Daughter*. ©2001 by Amy Tan.

At last, Old Widow Lau was done haggling with the driver and we stepped inside Father's shop. It was north-facing, quite dim inside, and perhaps this was why Father did not see us at first. He was busy with a customer, a man who was distinguished-looking, like the scholars of two decades before. The two men were bent over a glass case, discussing the different qualities of inksticks. Big Uncle welcomed us and invited us to be seated. From his formal tone, I knew he did not recognize who we were. So I called his name in a shy voice. And he squinted at me, then laughed and announced our arrival to Little Uncle, who apologized many times for not rushing over sooner to greet us. They rushed us to be seated at one of two tea tables for customers. Old Widow Lau refused their invitation three times, exclaiming that my father and uncles must be too busy for visitors. She made weak efforts to leave. On the fourth insistence, we finally sat. Then Little Uncle brought us hot tea and sweet oranges, as well as bamboo latticework fans with which to cool ourselves.

I tried to notice everything so I could later tell GaoLing what I had seen, and tease out her envy. The floors of the shop were of dark wood, polished and clean, no dirty footprints, even though this was during the dustiest part of the summer. And along the walls were display cases made of wood and glass. The glass was very shiny and not one pane was broken. Within those glass cases were our silk-wrapped boxes, all our hard work. They looked so much nicer than they had in the ink-making studio at Immortal Heart village.

I saw that Father had opened several of the boxes. He set sticks and cakes and other shapes on a silk cloth covering a glass case that served as a table on which he and the customer leaned. First he pointed to a stick with a top shaped like a fairy boat and said with graceful importance, "Your writing will flow as smoothly as a keel cutting through a glassy lake." He picked up a bird shape: "Your mind will soar into the

230

clouds of higher thought." He waved toward a row of ink cakes embellished with designs of peonies and bamboo: "Your ledgers will blossom into abundance while bamboo surrounds your quiet mind."

As he said this, Precious Auntie came back into mind. I was remembering how she taught me that everything, even ink, had a purpose and a meaning: Good ink cannot be the quick kind, ready to pour out of a bottle. You can never be an artist if your work comes without effort. That is the problem of modern ink from a bottle. You do not have to think. You simply write what is swimming on the top of your brain. And the top is nothing but pond scum, dead leaves, and mosquito spawn. But when you push an inkstick along an inkstone, you take the first step to cleansing your mind and your heart. You push and you ask yourself, What are my intentions? What is in my heart that matches my mind?

I remembered this, and yet that day in the ink shop, I listened to what Father was saying, and his words became far more important than anything Precious Auntie had thought. "Look here," Father said to his customer, and I looked. He held up an inkstick and rotated it in the light. "See? It's the right hue, purple-black, not brown or gray like the cheap brands you might find down the street. And listen to this." And I heard a sound as clean and pure as a small silver bell. "The high-pitched tone tells you that the soot is very fine, as smooth as the sliding banks of old rivers. And the scent—can you smell the balance of strength and delicacy, the musical notes of the ink's perfume? Expensive, and everyone who sees you using it will know that it was well worth the high price."

I was very proud to hear Father speak of our family's ink this way.

Post-Passage Questions

1. Do your SRS.

   (Actions: Yet again, the main action is a quick conversation. They come in, they sit down, and Old Widow Lau refuses a few times.)

2. Did Old Widow Lau want to leave and not stay for tea and oranges?

1. Something like: A girl walks into her family's ink shop and feels proud of the things her family creates.

2. No, she did not!

   Again here, as with the Nawabdin passage, Old Widow Lau is faking it.

   Old Widow Lau refuses three times and makes "weak efforts to leave". Weak efforts means she's not REALLY trying to leave.

   She also exclaims that "my father and uncles must be too busy for visitors." But, we know that there is only one customer in this shop…

   Don't just listen to what characters say!

Question 2

A main theme of the passage is that

    (A) family relationships should be nurtured.

    (B) quality is achieved through deliberate effort.

    (C) hard work results in material compensation.

    (D) creativity needs to be expressed concretely.

Find your evidence!

Every wrong answer here is due to Mental Gymnastics. You **could** say that the word "expensive" towards the end gets at the idea of "material compensation", or that family is clearly important to the narrator. But, the passage isn't about that in any huge way.

Ask yourself, "What would this look like if…?"

Correct answer is B.

Best Evidence: "Good ink cannot be the quick kind…You can never be an artist if your work comes without effort."

Question 4

It can be most reasonably inferred from the passage that Old Widow
Lau's reluctance to stay for tea is

(A) feigned, because she is not genuinely firm in her resolve.

(B) inconsiderate, because the family has been planning her visit.

(C) appropriate, because the shop is unusually busy.

(D) ill-advised, because she is exhausted from the journey.

Find your evidence!

Everyone gets this one wrong because Old Widow Lau is taken at her word. Most students pick C, but the disproof there we already know: There is only one customer in the shop.

Correct answer is A.

Best Evidence: She made "weak efforts to leave".

Nano Salt (Test 8)

Along with this passage, complete 3 MCAT passages.

You can take the full test 8 before reviewing these selected questions.

For every question you get wrong on test 8, physically write down a clear explanation of why the answer you picked was wrong. Then, take another guess for the correct answer. (This requires that you always write your answers on a separate sheet and grade them simply by marking them right or wrong. That way you will know if the question is wrong, but you won't know the correct answer.)

If you get more than 5 questions wrong on the reading section of test 8, you should come see me: CSnyder@VohraMethod.com. If you get fewer than 5 wrong, then you're on track. Keep working!

Read this passage and do your ridiculous summary. Then, we'll see if you understood the crux of this passage with a couple of questions!

This passage is adapted from Rachel Ehrenberg, "*Salt Stretches in Nanoworld.*" ©2009 by Society for Science & the Public. The "nanoworld" is the world observed on a scale one billionth that of ordinary human experience.

Inflexible old salt becomes a softy in the nanoworld, stretching like taffy to more than twice

its length, researchers report. The findings may lead to new approaches for making nanowires that could end up in solar cells or electronic circuits. The work also suggests that these ultra-tiny salt wires may already exist in sea spray and large underground salt deposits.

"We think nanowires are special and go to great lengths to make them," says study coauthor Nathan Moore of Sandia National Laboratories in Albuquerque. "Maybe they are more common than we think."

Metals such as gold or lead, in which bonding angles are loosey-goosey, can stretch out at temperatures well below their melting points. But scientists don't expect this superplasticity in a rigid, crystalline material like salt, Moore says.

This unusual behavior highlights that different forces rule the nanoworld, says theoretical physicist Krzysztof Kempa of Boston College. "Forget about gravity. It plays no role," he says. Surface tension and electrostatic forces are much more important at this scale.

Moore and his colleagues discovered salt's stretchiness accidently. They were investigating how water sticks to a surface such as salt and created a super-dry salt sample for testing. After cleaving a chunk of salt about the size of a sugar cube with a razor, the scientists guided a microscope that detects forces toward the surface. When the tip was far away there was no measured force, but within about seven nanometers a very strong attraction rapidly developed between the diamond tip of the microscope and the salt. The salt actually stretched out to glom on to the microscope tip. Using an electron microscope to see what was happening, the researchers observed the nanowires.

240

The initial attraction between the tip and salt might be due to electrostatic forces, perhaps good old van der Waals interactions[1], the researchers speculate. Several mechanisms might lead to the elasticity, including the excessive surface tension found in the nanoworld (the same tension that allows a water strider to skim the surface of a pond).

The surface tension is so strong that as the microscope pulls away from the salt, the salt stretches, Kempa says. "The inside has no choice but to rearrange the atoms, rather than break," he says.

This bizarre behavior is actually mirrored in the macroworld, the researchers say. Huge underground deposits of salt can bend like plastic, but water is believed to play a role at these scales. Perhaps salty nanowires are present in these deposits as well.

"Sodium chloride[2] is everywhere—in the air, in our bodies," Moore says. "This may change our view of things, of what's happening at the nanoscale."

The work also suggests new techniques for making nanowires, which are often created through nano-imprinting techniques, Kempa says. "We invoke the intuition of the macroworld," he says. "Maybe instead of stamping [nanowires] we should be nano-pulling them."

[1] Attractive forces between nearby atoms
[2] Common salt

Interaction of Microscope Tip with Salt Surface

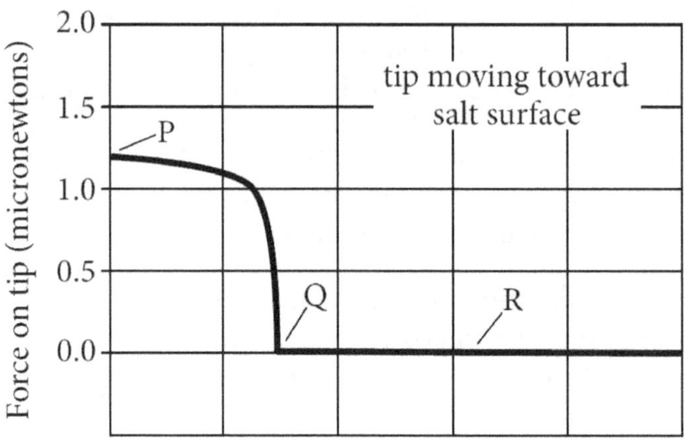

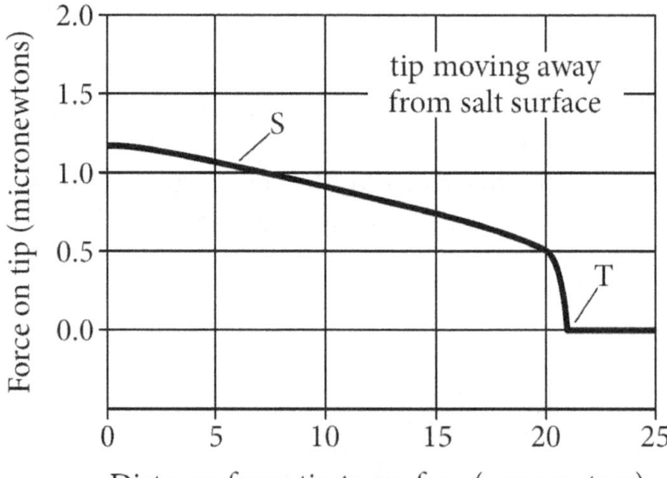

Adapted from Moore et al., "Superplastic Nanowires Pulled from the Surface of Common Salt." ©2009 by American Chemical Society.

Post-Passage Questions

1. Do your SRS.
   (Look for any opinions!)

2. Describe in detail what those two graphs are showing you. Turn the numbers and lines into simple words. Actually write it down!

Answers:

1. Something like this: "Scientists be like, Oops! We made salt be stretchy. Maybe we can use it for stuff."
   (By the way, if your SRSs still need work, contact me today. Your SRS should be really close to mine at this point. If yours is much longer or has a lot more detail or feels a lot more dense, then you need to work on that as soon as possible! CSnyder@VohraMethod.com)

   There aren't any opinions in this passage. At best, there are things like hypotheses or conjectures. Those aren't the same thing.

Before I give you the answer for 2, I want you to try out this question:

Question 31

Based on the passage and the graph, which label on the graph indicates the point at which a salt nanowire breaks?

(A) P
(B) Q
(C) R
(D) T

Write down your answer and your logic.

Okay, let's describe our graphs in detail now.

First key idea: The top graph should be read from right to left. If the tip is moving **towards** the salt, then you would think of it as starting at 25 nanometers away and then moving closer (aka left).

This is just logic, but most students keep the passages so distant that they don't ever notice something as simple as this. Don't let that be you!

So, reading it right to left, we see that there is no force measured between the tip and the salt until around 7 nanometers away, at which point the force quickly builds up and then levels off to hit 1.2ish when the tip is touching the salt. In the passage, this is described as when the salt "actually stretched out to glom on to the microscope tip."

The second graph can be read left to right. We start off with the force at that same 1.2ish micronewtons and the tip touching the salt. As we pull the tip away from the salt, the force gradually decreases all the way out to around 20 nanometers. Then the force quickly decreases until there is no longer any force between the salt and the tip.

This makes sense because they salt would be stretching that entire time. Imagine if you had silly putty or taffy or something. If you pull it apart at two ends, it would stretch out. The connective forces would weaken more and more until eventually the putty or taffy strand would break near the middle and the two ends would fall (zero force).

In the passage, we are told that "the surface tension is so strong that as the microscope pulls away from the salt, the salt stretches."

Thus, the break point would be point T.

Most students end up either getting T because they guessed, or they end up picking a letter from the completely wrong graph. This is why it's important to think about what the graphs are telling you. When the tip is moving towards the salt, there would NOT be any breakage. The connection between salt and tip hasn't occurred yet. They are just two separated things with no force between them.

However, when the tip is moving away, salt stretches (we know this also from the passage). In that case, something that is stretching will always, eventually, break. It only makes sense for the breakage to happen in the second graph. By that fact of logic alone you could get this question correct.

Stay alert! And make sure you understand what every graph and chart on the SAT is telling you.

Question 24

Which choice provides the best evidence for the claim that Moore's group was surprised to observe salt stretching?

(A) Lines 17-18 ("But . . . says")
(B) Lines 26-28 ("They were . . . testing")
(C) Lines 36-38 ("Using . . . nanowires")
(D) Lines 55-56 ("Sodium . . . says")

I don't know that this one is SO hard, but I want to use it to reinforce a point. Surprise is really easy to see. In order to have surprise, you have to have people NOT know a thing, and then figure it out. You will see things like "discovered by accident". You'll see words like "unexpected".

Surprise is never some super hidden thing that takes a lot of effort to find in the passage. Nothing on the SAT really is.

Answer is A.

Questions 26

According to the passage, researchers have identified which mechanism as potentially responsible for the initial attraction between the microscope tip and the salt?

- **(A)** Gravity
- **(B)** Nano-imprinting
- **(C)** Surface tension
- **(D)** Van der Waals interactions

Find your evidence!

This one should be so simple, and yet most students get it wrong. This is just pure evidence finding.

Answer is D.

Best Evidence: The initial attraction between the tip and salt might be due to electrostatic forces, perhaps good old van der Waals interactions, the researchers speculate.

It's nearly word for word.

Don't just answer questions based on the words you think you remember hearing in the passage, out of context! **That is very obviously not smart.** Just find each word in the passage and read the given information about each one. The "surface tension" is mentioned in the passage as possibly causing the **"elasticity"**, NOT as possibly causing the "initial attraction between the microscope tip and the salt".

Question 28

Based on the passage, which choice best describes the relationship between salt behavior in the nanoworld and in the macroworld?

(A) In both the nanoworld and the macroworld, salt can be flexible.

(B) Salt flexibility is expected in the nanoworld but is surprising in the macroworld.

(C) Salt nanowires were initially observed in the nanoworld and later observed in the macroworld.

(D) In the nanoworld, salt's interactions with water lead to very different properties than they do in the macroworld.

Answer and find your evidence!!

Answer is A.

Best Evidence: "Huge underground deposits of salt can bend like plastic, but water is believed to play a role at these scales."

D is the main trick answer here. D is wrong because we have no idea how salt interacts with water in the nanoworld. In fact, the researchers specifically created "super-dry salt" for their experiment with the microscope tip. We do hear about salt interacting with water in the macroworld, but that evidence is what proves A, not D.

Higgs Boson Passage (Test 7)

Along with this passage, complete 3 MCAT passages.

You can take the full test 7 before reviewing these selected questions.

For every question you get wrong on test 7, physically write down a clear explanation of why the answer you picked was wrong. Then, take another guess for the correct answer. (This requires that you always write your answers on a separate sheet and grade them simply by marking them right or wrong. That way you will know if the question is wrong, but you won't know the correct answer.)

If you get more than 4 questions wrong on the reading section of test 7, you should come see me: CSnyder@VohraMethod.com. If you get fewer than 4 wrong, then you're on track. Keep working!

Read this passage and do your ridiculous summary. Then, we'll see if you understood the crux of this passage with a couple of questions!

This passage is adapted from Brian Greene, "*How the Higgs Boson Was Found.*" ©2013 by Smithsonian Institution. The Higgs boson is an elementary particle associated with the Higgs field. Experiments conducted in 2012–2013 tentatively confirmed the existence of the Higgs boson and thus of the Higgs field.

Nearly a half-century ago, Peter Higgs and a handful of other physicists were trying to understand the origin of a basic physical feature: mass. You can think of mass as an object's heft or, a little more precisely, as the resistance it offers to having its motion changed. Push on a freight train (or a feather) to increase its speed, and the resistance you feel reflects its mass. At a microscopic level, the freight train's mass comes from its constituent molecules and atoms, which are themselves built from fundamental particles, electrons and quarks. But where do the masses of these and other fundamental particles come from?

When physicists in the 1960s modeled the behavior of these particles using equations rooted in quantum physics, they encountered a puzzle. If they imagined that the particles were all massless, then each term in the equations clicked into a perfectly symmetric pattern, like the tips of a perfect snowflake. And this symmetry was not just mathematically elegant. It explained patterns evident in the experimental data. But—and here's the puzzle—physicists knew that the particles did have mass, and when they modified the equations to account for this fact, the mathematical harmony was spoiled. The equations became complex and unwieldy and, worse still, inconsistent.

What to do? Here's the idea put forward by Higgs. Don't shove the particles' masses down the throat of the beautiful equations. Instead, keep the equations pristine and symmetric, but consider them operating within a peculiar environment. Imagine that all of space is uniformly filled with an invisible substance—now called the Higgs field—that exerts a drag force on particles when they accelerate through it. Push on a fundamental particle in an effort to increase its speed and, according to Higgs, you would feel this drag force as a resistance. Justifiably, you would interpret the resistance as the particle's mass. For a mental toehold, think of a ping-pong ball submerged in water. When you push on the ping-pong ball, it will feel much more massive than it does outside of water. Its interaction with the watery environment has the effect of endowing it with mass. So with particles submerged in the Higgs field.

In 1964, Higgs submitted a paper to a prominent physics journal in which he formulated this idea mathematically. The paper was rejected. Not because it contained a technical error, but because the premise of an invisible something permeating space, interacting with particles to provide their mass, well, it all just seemed like heaps of overwrought speculation. The editors of the journal deemed it "of no obvious relevance to physics."

But Higgs persevered (and his revised paper appeared later that year in another journal), and physicists who took the time to study the proposal gradually realized that his idea was a stroke of genius, one that allowed them to have their cake and eat it too. In Higgs's scheme, the fundamental equations can retain their pristine form because the dirty work of providing the particles' masses is relegated to the environment.

While I wasn't around to witness the initial rejection of Higgs's proposal in 1964 (well, I was around, but only barely), I can attest that by the mid-1980s, the assessment had changed. The physics community had, for the most part, fully bought into the idea that there was a Higgs field permeating space. In fact, in a graduate course I took that covered what's known as the Standard Model of Particle Physics (the quantum equations physicists have assembled to describe the particles of matter and the dominant forces by which they influence each other), the professor presented the Higgs field with such certainty that for a long while I had no idea it had yet to be established experimentally. On occasion, that happens in physics. Mathematical equations can sometimes tell such a convincing tale, they can seemingly radiate reality so strongly, that they become entrenched in the vernacular of working physicists, even before there's data to confirm them.

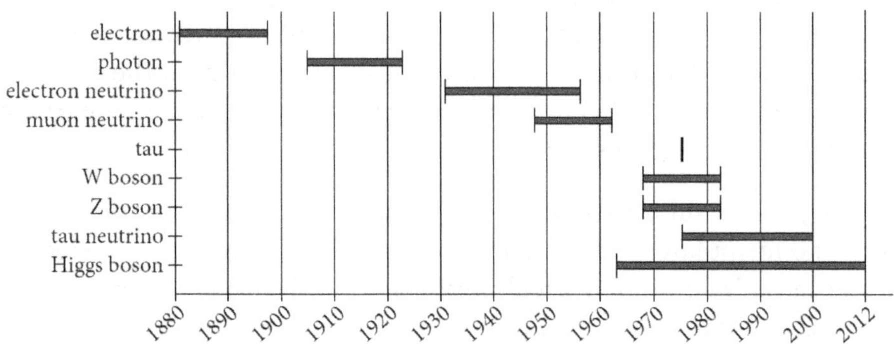

Adapted from the editors of *The Economist*, "Worth the Wait." ©2012 by The Economist Newspaper Limited.

1. Do your SRS.
    (Find any opinions!)

2. Explain the problem that Higgs was trying to solve.

1. Something like this:

    Higgs be like, "We could solve our problems by making the particles not have mass and making up some 'stuff' around the particles that would have the mass." At first, everyone thought his idea was silly.

    This one is a bit hard to simplify, I got you. But, still try to make it silly not NOT dense!

    Opinions: There is one. "…it all just seemed like heaps of overwrought speculation." That opinion will come up in the questions!

2. The problem is that all the equations are wonderful and pretty and work, but only IF you make the assumption that the particles have no mass. But, we know that the particles must have mass. So, that assumption is false. Meaning we would need all new equations…or something. (That's where Higgs comes in.)

Question 44

The author most strongly suggests that the reason the scientific community initially rejected Higgs's idea was that the idea

1. addressed a problem unnoticed by other physicists.
2. only worked if the equations were flawless.
3. rendered accepted theories in physics obsolete.
4. appeared to have little empirical basis.

Find your evidence!

Other physicists definitely noticed; they had been discussing the problem for a while. (not A)

The equations already **were** flawless…assuming the particles had no mass. That was the key problem. (not B)

Higgs's theory actually helped to reconcile the existing problem; it didn't make anything obsolete. (not C)

Answer is D. Mostly, you can get this one just through logic.

Best Evidence: "Not because it contained a technical error, but because the premise of an invisible something permeating space, interacting with particles to provide their mass, well, it all just **seemed like heaps of overwrought speculation**."

To be fair, Higgs WAS just speculating…

Also to be fair, most of **theoretical** physics is speculation for a long time before it gets proved.

Question 46

The author notes that one reason Higgs's theory gained acceptance was that it

- **(A)** let scientists accept two conditions that had previously seemed irreconcilable.
- **(B)** introduced an innovative approach that could be applied to additional problems.
- **(C)** answered a question that earlier scientists had not even raised.
- **(D)** explained why two distinct phenomena were being misinterpreted as one phenomenon.

Find your evidence!

Remember, your evidence is the most important part of your answer. Getting one question right just proves that you can get that question right. Proving that your answer is right shows that you can get similar questions right in the future.

Answer is A.

Best Evidence: "But Higgs persevered (and his revised paper appeared later that year in another journal), and physicists who took the time to study the proposal gradually realized that his idea was a stroke of genius, one that allowed them to have their cake and eat it too. In Higgs's scheme, **the fundamental equations can retain their pristine form because the dirty work of providing the particles' masses is relegated to the environment.**"

Question 48

Which statement best describes the technique the author uses to advance the main point of the last paragraph?

- **(A)** He recounts a personal experience to illustrate a characteristic of the discipline of physics.
- **(B)** He describes his own education to show how physics has changed during his career.
- **(C)** He provides autobiographical details to demonstrate how Higgs's theory was confirmed.
- **(D)** He contrasts the status of Higgs's theory at two time periods to reveal how the details of the theory evolved.

Find your evidence and write down a brief explanation.

I include this one because A, B, and C are so similar at the start. "Recounting a personal experience" and "providing autobiographical details" are definitely different, but they sound very same-y. "Describing his own education" also sounds just like autobiographical stuff.

Do we, then, use the "SAT guessing method" and pick D?

No, don't be silly. We don't need guessing!

You have a couple options:

1. Ask yourself what the first half of each answer choice would look like.
2. Focus primarily on the second halves of each answer choice.

I don't really mind which you choose. Either way, go ahead and disprove every wrong answer choice (or, whichever ones you didn't pick).

B is wrong. Physics didn't change. At least, that's not what the last paragraph is saying. It's talking about how Physics tends to adopt an idea and believe in it long before it gets scientifically proven. That's a similarity between physics decades ago and physics today.

C is wrong. The only real "autobiographical detail" we get is that he went to graduate school… That's not detailed. Also, we have no idea how Higgs's theory was confirmed. That's not in this passage.

D is wrong. In this passage, we don't see any change in the details of Higgs's theory. We are only told that he submitted a "revised paper" a little later in the year he was initially rejected. Again, that's not "details".

A is correct. The "discipline of physics" is that people talk about theories as if they were proven true, long before they actually are.

Best Evidence: "On occasion, that happens in physics. Mathematical equations can sometimes tell such a convincing tale, they can seemingly radiate reality so strongly, that they become entrenched in the vernacular of working physicists, even before there's data to confirm them."

Question 52

Based on the graph, the author's depiction of Higgs's theory in the mid-1980s is most analogous to which hypothetical situation?

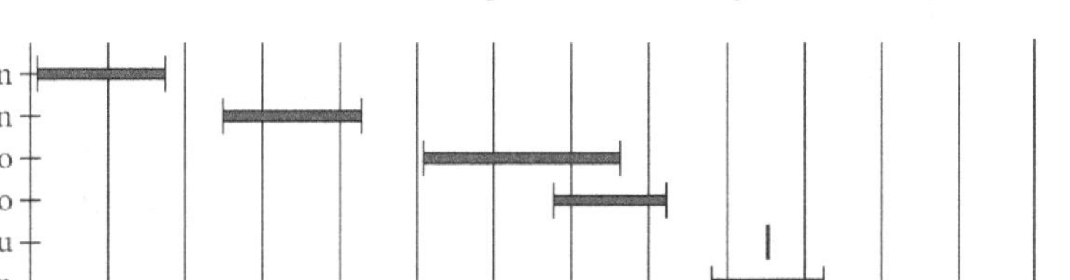

Adapted from the editors of *The Economist*, "Worth the Wait." ©2012 by The Economist Newspaper Limited.

(A) The muon neutrino was widely disputed until being confirmed in the early 1960s.

(B) Few physicists in 2012 doubted the reality of the tau neutrino.

(C) No physicists prior to 1960 considered the possibility of the W or Z boson.

(D) Most physicists in 1940 believed in the existence of the electron neutrino.

Find your evidence!

Best Evidence: "I can attest that by the mid-1980s, the assessment had changed. The physics community had, for the most part, fully bought into the idea that there was a Higgs field permeating space."

So, people believed in Higgs's theory as early as the 80s, even though it wasn't proved until 2012-2013.

Answer choice D is correct here. The electron neutrino wasn't proved until 1956 or 1957, based on this graph. So, if most physicists believed in the electron neutrino's existence in 1940, that would match how they viewed Higgs's theory before it was proved!

Waves (Test 2)

Along with this passage, complete 3 MCAT passages.

You can take the full test 2 before reviewing these selected questions.

For every question you get wrong on test 2, physically write down a clear explanation of why the answer you picked was wrong. Then, take another guess for the correct answer. (This requires that you always write your answers on a separate sheet and grade them simply by marking them right or wrong. That way you will know if the question is wrong, but you won't know the correct answer.)

If you get more than 3 questions wrong on the reading section of test 2, you should come see me: CSnyder@VohraMethod.com. If you get fewer than 3 wrong, then you're on track. Keep working!

Read this passage and do your ridiculous summary. Then, we'll see if you understood the crux of this passage with a couple of questions!

This passage is adapted from Geoffrey Giller, *"Long a Mystery, How 500-Meter-High Undersea Waves Form Is Revealed."* ©2014 by Scientific American.

Some of the largest ocean waves in the world are nearly impossible to see. Unlike other large waves, these rollers, called internal waves, do not ride the ocean surface. Instead, they move underwater, undetectable without the use of satellite imagery or sophisticated monitoring equipment. Despite their hidden nature, internal waves are fundamental parts of ocean water dynamics, transferring heat to the ocean depths and bringing up cold water from below.

And they can reach staggering heights—some as tall as skyscrapers.

Because these waves are involved in ocean mixing and thus the transfer of heat, understanding them is crucial to global climate modeling, says Tom Peacock, a researcher at the Massachusetts Institute of Technology. Most models fail to take internal waves into account. "If we want to have more and more accurate climate models, we have to be able to capture processes such as this," Peacock says.

Peacock and his colleagues tried to do just that. Their study, published in November in *Geophysical Research Letters*, focused on internal waves generated in the Luzon Strait, which separates Taiwan and the Philippines. Internal waves in this region, thought to be some of the largest in the world, can reach about 500 meters high. "That's the same height as the Freedom Tower that's just been built in New York," Peacock says.

Although scientists knew of this phenomenon in the South China Sea and beyond, they didn't know exactly how internal waves formed. To find out, Peacock and a team of researchers from M.I.T. and Woods Hole Oceanographic Institution worked with France's National Center for Scientific Research using a giant facility there called the Coriolis Platform. The rotating platform, about 15 meters (49.2 feet) in diameter, turns at variable speeds and can simulate Earth's rotation. It also has walls, which means scientists can fill it with water and create accurate, large-scale simulations of various oceanographic scenarios.

Peacock and his team built a carbon-fiber resin scale model of the Luzon Strait, including the islands and surrounding ocean floor topography. Then they filled the platform with water of varying salinity to replicate the different densities found at the strait, with denser, saltier water below and lighter, less briny water above. Small particles were added to the solution and illuminated with lights from below in order to track how the liquid moved. Finally, they re-created tides using two large plungers to see how the internal waves themselves formed.

The Luzon Strait's underwater topography, with a distinct double-ridge shape, turns out to be responsible for generating the underwater waves. As the tide rises and falls and water moves through the strait, colder, denser water is pushed up over the ridges into warmer, less dense layers above it. This action results in bumps of colder water trailed by warmer water that generate an internal wave. As these waves move toward land, they become steeper—much the same way waves at the beach become taller before they hit the shore—until they break on a continental shelf.

The researchers were also able to devise a mathematical model that describes the movement and formation of these waves. Whereas the model is specific to the Luzon Strait, it can still help researchers understand how internal waves are generated in other places around the world. Eventually, this information will be incorporated into global climate models, making them more accurate. "It's very clear, within the context of these [global climate] models, that internal waves play a role in driving ocean circulations," Peacock says.

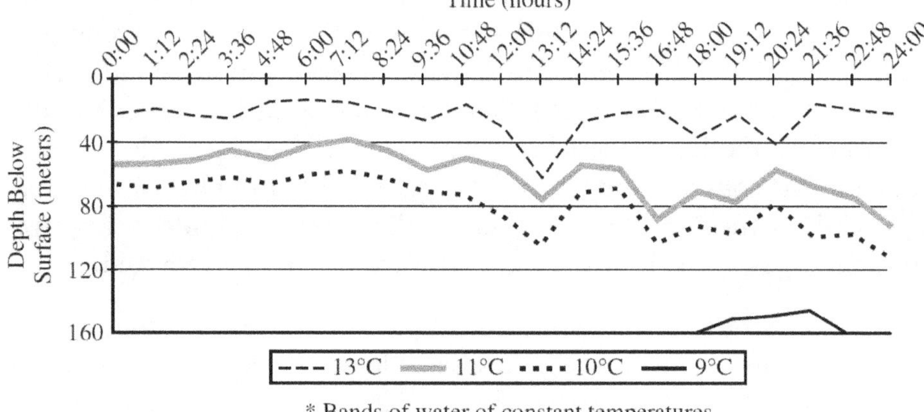

Adapted from Justin Small et al., "Internal Solitons in the Ocean: Prediction from SAR." ©1998 by Oceanography, Defence Evaluation and Research Agency.

Post-Passage Questions

1. Do your SRS.
2. Find any opinions!
3. What happened in the graph at 1:12pm (13:12)?

1. Something like this:

    Some scientists be like, "Let's measure underwater waves so we can help save the planet."

2. This is the closest we get to an opinion in this passage: "If we want to have more and more accurate climate models, we have to be able to capture processes such as this," Peacock says.

3. Something (probably an internal wave) pushed the warmer layers of water down, then they came back up.

Question 45

According to Peacock, the ability to monitor internal waves is significant primarily because

- **(A)** it will allow scientists to verify the maximum height of such waves.
- **(B)** it will allow researchers to shift their focus to improving the quality of satellite images.
- **(C)** the study of wave patterns will enable regions to predict and prevent coastal damage.
- **(D)** the study of such waves will inform the development of key scientific models.

Find your evidence!

This question is asking for Peacock's opinion. So, your evidence is that opinion you pulled out earlier.

"If we want to have more and more accurate climate models, we have to be able to capture processes such as this."

Answer is D.

Question 48

Based on information in the passage, it can reasonably be inferred that all internal waves

- **(A)** reach approximately the same height even though the locations and depths of continental shelves vary.
- **(B)** may be caused by similar factors but are influenced by the distinct topographies of different regions.
- **(C)** can be traced to inconsistencies in the tidal patterns of deep ocean water located near islands.
- **(D)** are generated by the movement of dense water over a relatively flat section of the ocean floor.

Inference does NOT mean "guess wildly and don't look for evidence in the passage at all." Inference means "go get some clear, direct textual evidence that supports your answer choice, just like every other question!"

Find your evidence.

Answer is B. If you picked any of the other ones, go find evidence in the passage now that disproves whatever you picked.

Best Evidence for B: "Whereas the model is specific to the Luzon Strait, it can still help researchers understand how internal waves are generated in other places around the world."

Evidence against A: Line 10: "And they can reach staggering heights—some as tall as skyscrapers."

Line 24: "Internal waves in this region, thought to be some of the largest in the world, can reach about 500 meters high."

Both of these show that these waves CAN be very big, SOME as tall as skyscrapers. That means that SOME are not that tall. They are not all the same height.

Evidence against C: This one is a weird wrong answer. Although the passage does discuss the impact of tides, it's not talking about any "inconsistencies" in those tides.

Evidence against D: Line 53 (and the rest of that paragraph): "The Luzon Strait's underwater topography, with a distinct double-ridge shape, turns out to be responsible for generating the underwater waves." It's caused by the ridges, not flat ocean floor.

Question 50

In the graph, which isotherm displays an increase in depth below the surface during the period 19:12 to 20:24?

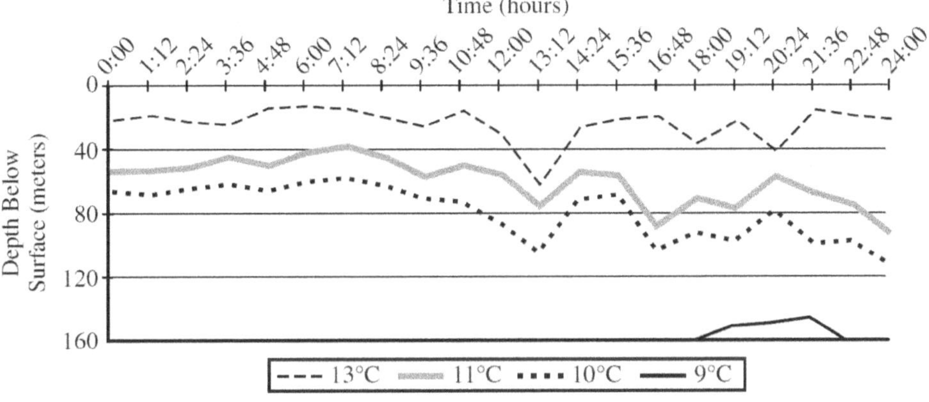

* Bands of water of constant temperatures

Adapted from Justin Small et al., "Internal Solitons in the Ocean: Prediction from SAR." ©1998 by Oceanography, Defence Evaluation and Research Agency.

(A) 9°C

(B) 10°C

(C) 11°C

(D) 13°C

The only way you really get this one wrong is if you misread "increase in depth" as "going up on the graph". Increase in depth means that you would be getting deepER and would thus be going **down** on the graph.

Question 51

Which concept is supported by the passage and by the information in the graph?

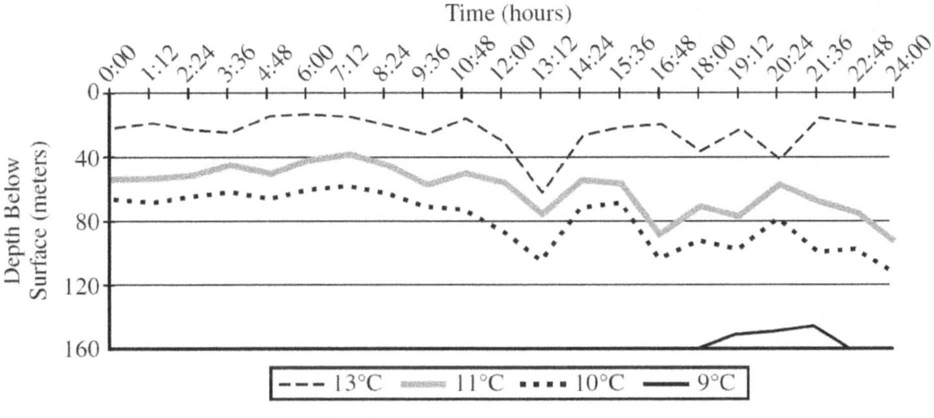

* Bands of water of constant temperatures

Adapted from Justin Small et al., "Internal Solitons in the Ocean: Prediction from SAR." ©1998 by Oceanography, Defence Evaluation and Research Agency.

- **(A)** Internal waves cause water of varying salinity to mix.
- **(B)** Internal waves push denser water above layers of less dense water.
- **(C)** Internal waves push bands of cold water above bands of warmer water.
- **(D)** Internal waves do not rise to break the ocean's surface.

For this question, you can focus solely on the graph. This graph is limited. ALL graphs are limited. They don't just tell you everything in the whole world.

This graph shows us patches of water at different temperatures and how deep those patches are. This graph does NOT show us salinity. It does NOT show us density. And, on this particular graph, the colder bands of water never cross above the warmer bands.

So, D is our answer.

Really pay attention to the limitations of your data, charts, and graphs in science passages!

Question 52

How does the graph support the author's point that internal waves affect ocean water dynamics?

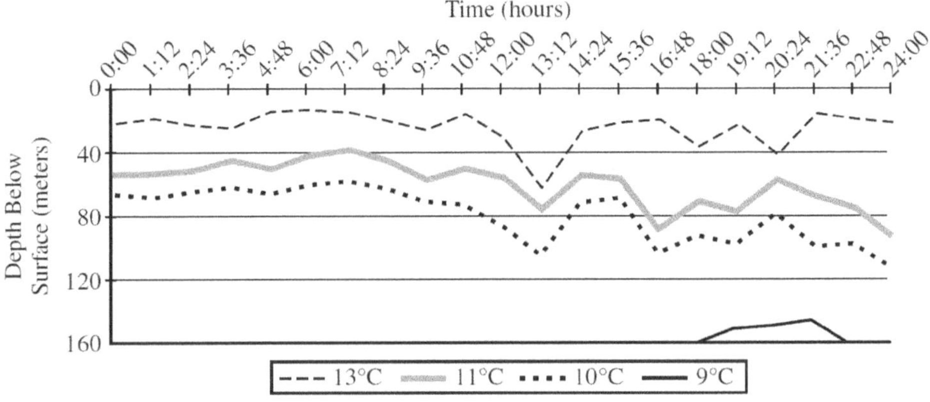

Adapted from Justin Small et al., "Internal Solitons in the Ocean: Prediction from SAR." ©1998 by Oceanography, Defence Evaluation and Research Agency.

(A) It demonstrates that wave movement forces warmer water down to depths that typically are colder.

(B) It reveals the degree to which an internal wave affects the density of deep layers of cold water.

(C) It illustrates the change in surface temperature that takes place during an isolated series of deep waves.

(D) It shows that multiple waves rising near the surface of the ocean disrupt the flow of normal tides.

Immediately reinforcing the same point: Limitations of the graph.

This graph does not show density. It does not show surface temperature. It does not tell us anything about tides. You don't even have to look at the passage at all in this case. Only one answer is true of the graph at all, and that is A.

Wisdom of crowds (Test 5)

Along with this passage, complete 4 MCAT passages.

You can take the full test 5 before reviewing these selected questions. I have included one other passage from test 5. It is the dual passages one, and it is the next passage after this.

For every question you get wrong on test 5, physically write down a clear explanation of why the answer you picked was wrong. Then, take another guess for the correct answer. (This requires that you always write your answers on a separate sheet and grade them simply by marking them right or wrong. That way you will know if the question is wrong, but you won't know the correct answer.)

If you get more than 2 questions wrong on the reading section of test 5, you should come see me: CSnyder@VohraMethod.com. If you get fewer than 2 wrong, then you're on track. Keep working!

Read this passage and do your ridiculous summary. Then, we'll see if you understood the crux of this passage with a couple of questions!

This passage is adapted from John Bohannon, "*Why You Shouldn't Trust Internet Comments.*" ©2013 by American Association for the Advancement of Science.

The "wisdom of crowds" has become a mantra of the Internet age. Need to choose a new vacuum cleaner? Check out the reviews on online merchant Amazon. But a new study suggests that such online scores don't always reveal the best choice. A massive controlled experiment of Web users finds that such ratings are highly susceptible to irrational "herd behavior"—and that the herd can be manipulated.

Sometimes the crowd really is wiser than you. The classic examples are guessing the weight of a bull or the number of gumballs in a jar. Your guess is probably going to be far from the mark, whereas the average of many people's choices is remarkably close to the true number.

But what happens when the goal is to judge something less tangible, such as the quality or worth of a product? According to one theory, the wisdom of the crowd still holds—measuring the aggregate of people's opinions produces a stable, reliable value. Skeptics, however, argue that people's opinions are easily swayed by those of others. So nudging a crowd early on by presenting contrary opinions—for example, exposing them to some very good or very bad attitudes—will steer the crowd in a different direction. To test which hypothesis is true, you would need to manipulate huge numbers of people, exposing them to false information and determining how it affects their opinions.

A team led by Sinan Aral, a network scientist at the Massachusetts Institute of Technology in Cambridge, did exactly that. Aral has been secretly working with a popular website that aggregates news stories. The website allows users to make comments about news stories and vote each other's comments up or down. The vote tallies are visible as a number next to each comment, and the position of the comments is chronological. (Stories on the site get an average of about ten comments and about three votes per comment.) It's a follow-up to his experiment using people's ratings of movies to measure how much individual people influence each other online (answer: a lot). This time, he wanted to know how much the crowd influences the individual, and whether it can be controlled from outside.

For five months, every comment submitted by a user randomly received an "up" vote (positive); a "down" vote (negative); or as a control, no vote at all. The team then observed how users rated those comments. The users generated more than 100,000 comments that were viewed more than 10 million times and rated more than 300,000 times by other users.

At least when it comes to comments on news sites, the crowd is more herdlike than wise. Comments that received fake positive votes from the researchers were 32% more likely to receive more positive votes compared with a control, the team reports. And those comments were no more likely than the control to be down-voted by the next viewer to see them. By the end of the study, positively manipulated comments got an overall boost of about 25%. However, the same did not hold true for negative manipulation. The ratings of comments that got a fake down vote were usually negated by an up vote by the next user to see them.

"Our experiment does not reveal the psychology behind people's decisions," Aral says, "but an intuitive explanation is that people are more skeptical of negative social influence. They're more willing to go along with positive opinions from other people."

Duncan Watts, a network scientist at Microsoft Research in New York City, agrees with that conclusion. "[But] one question is whether the positive [herding] bias is specific to this site" or true in general, Watts says. He points out that the category of the news items in the experiment had a strong effect on how much people could be manipulated. "I would have thought that 'business' is pretty similar to 'economics,' yet they find a much stronger effect (almost 50% stronger) for the former than the latter. What explains this difference? If we're going to apply these findings in the real world, we'll need to know the answers."

Will companies be able to boost their products by manipulating on-line ratings on a massive scale? "That is easier said than done," Watts says. If people detect—or learn—that comments on a website are being manipulated, the herd may spook and leave entirely.

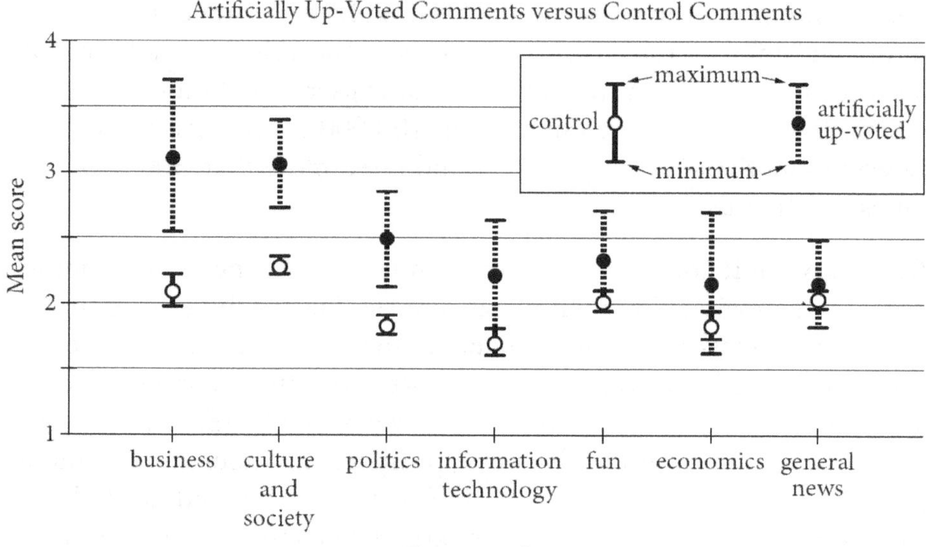

Mean score: mean of scores for the comments in each category, with the score for each comment being determined by the number of positive votes from website users minus the number of negative votes.

Adapted from Lev Muchnik, Sinan Aral, and Sean J. Taylor, "*Social Influence Bias: A Randomized Experiment.*" 2013 by American Association for the Advancement of Science.

Post-Passage Questions

1. Do your SRS.
2. Are there any opinions up in here?
3. What is the biggest limitation of this study? (There is textual
    evidence for this answer!)

1. Something like this:
Some scientists be like, "Can we change peoples' minds by pretending that other people think positively or negatively of a thing?" (aka, can we create herd behavior?)

2. There are several hypotheses and scientific questions. All that is not the same as a raw opinion. Aral does have this opinion:

    "…an **intuitive** explanation is that people are more skeptical of negative social influence. They're more willing to go along with positive opinions from other people." "Intuitive" is an opinion word.

3. The biggest limitation is that the study doesn't tell us the internal thoughts, motivations, or decision-making process of any of the people in the study. We know THAT people responded a certain way, but we have no idea WHY they did that. The lack of the WHY is the primary concern of the last two paragraphs, actually. So, this is a big part of the passage.

    Evidence: "Our experiment does not reveal the psychology behind people's decisions…"

    Also: "If we're going to apply these findings in the real world, we'll need to know the answers." (to questions about the peoples' motivations).

    In general, asking yourself about any limitations in a science passage is a good idea. The SAT loves to include answer choices that go beyond what the study could possibly prove or beyond what the graph says, etc.

Question 33

The author of the passage suggests that crowds may be more effective at

(A) creating controversy than examining an issue in depth.

(B) reinforcing members' ideas than challenging those ideas.

(C) arriving at accurate quantitative answers than producing valid qualitative judgments.

(D) ranking others' opinions than developing genuinely original positions.

Find your evidence!

Most students who get this wrong pick B. If you picked B, take a minute to think about why B is definitely wrong. Write it down.

B is saying that people are good at reinforcing each other, but not good at challenging each other. But, the study in this passage was only trying to figure out how much people could be influenced by each other. Being influenced by others' opinions is very different from reinforcing them.

And, sure it says that the people were not as influenced by the randomized, artificial down-vote. But, that doesn't mean that they are bad at challenging ideas. Again, the biggest limitation of this study is that we don't know anything that's going on in these peoples' heads. We don't know why they choose to up-vote or down-vote or not vote or anything.

So, B is a trick answer because it just vaguely sounds like some similar ideas. Don't fall for vague!!

Now, C is the correct answer. If you haven't already, pick your evidence to support C.

In these cases, ideally you want evidence that supports BOTH concepts. So, evidence showing that people are good at quantitative **and** bad at qualitative.

Feel free to find two separate pieces of evidence if you can't find one sentence together (as a general rule). But, always look for one spot that proves both together (also as a general rule!).

Best Evidence for Good at Quantitative: "Your guess is probably going to be far from the mark, whereas the average of many people's choices is remarkably close to the true number."

Best Evidence for Bad at Qualitative: "A massive controlled experiment of Web users finds that such ratings are highly susceptible to irrational "herd behavior"—and that the herd can be manipulated." (That's a good summary of the whole passage!)

Now, for some reason a lot of students end up picking this evidence in the subsequent evidence question: "According to one theory, the wisdom of the crowd still holds—measuring the aggregate of people's opinions produces a stable, reliable value."

Just in case you picked that, I will note that that evidence suggests that people are GOOD at qualitative, not bad at it. It's just one theory, and it's also not the author's theory (Question 33 asks about the author's thoughts). But regardless, it proves the exact wrong thing.

Question 35

Which choice best supports the view of the "skeptics" (Line 20)?

(A) "Comments that received fake positive votes from the researchers were 32% more likely to receive more positive votes compared with a control, the team reports."

(B) "And those comments were no more likely than the control to
be down-voted by the next viewer to see them."

(C) "The ratings of comments that got a fake down vote were usually negated by an up vote by the next user to see them."

(D) "He points out that the category of the news items in the
experiment had a strong effect on how much people could be
manipulated."

Most students narrow it down to A and D. Let's look at the difference.

The view of the skeptics is that "people's opinions are easily swayed by those of others".

D, when viewed alone, takes for granted the idea that people can be manipulated and jumps into how much they can be manipulated in different contexts.

A shows clear evidence that people can be manipulated.

Which of those helps to prove that people can be manipulated? A is the answer.

I know D has the word manipulated in it, but A is far more direct. It clearly states the thing we want to prove. We like direct.

Question 41

Data presented in the figure most directly support which idea from the passage?

- **(A)** The mean score of artificially down-voted comments is similar to that of the control.
- **(B)** The patterns observed in the experiment suggest that people are suspicious of negative social influence.
- **(C)** The positive bias observed in users of the news site may not apply to human behavior in other contexts.
- **(D)** The type of story being commented on has an impact on the degree to which people can be influenced.

Looking ONLY at the graph, here's what we see.

The title of the graph is "Artificially **Up-Voted** Comments versus Control Comments". Meaning, this graph doesn't tell us about **down-voted** comments. So, A is out.

B is wrong because, remember, our biggest limitation in this study is that we have NO IDEA what people are thinking. We don't know if they are suspicious or any other emotion. And the graph certainly cannot convey suspicion…

C was definitely a concern that Watts mentioned, but just looking at the chart we have no way of knowing that some random other contexts (not featured here) might be impacted in different ways…

D is correct. This graph shows different types of stories (business vs politics vs fun…), and it clearly shows that the influence is different. For example, business stories were far more impacted than either economics or general news. Watts also mentions this in the last two paragraphs of the passage.

Reminder: Pay attention to what data in a graph **can actually, possibly prove.**

Beecher vs Grimke Dual Passage (Test 5)

If you are a boy, you must read this section!

Along with this passage, complete 4 MCAT passages.

You can take the full test 5 before reviewing these selected questions. I have included one other passage from test 5. It is the dual passages one, and it is the next passage after this.

For every question you get wrong on test 5, physically write down a clear explanation of why the answer you picked was wrong. Then, take another guess for the correct answer. (This requires that you always write your answers on a separate sheet and grade them simply by marking them right or wrong. That way you will know if the question is wrong, but you won't know the correct answer.)

If you get more than 2 questions wrong on the reading section of test 5, you should come see me: CSnyder@VohraMethod.com. If you get fewer than 2 wrong, then you're on track. Keep working!

Read this passage and do your ridiculous summary. Then, we'll see if you understood the crux of this passage with a couple of questions!

Passage 1 is adapted from Catharine Beecher, *Essay on Slavery and Abolitionism*. Originally published in 1837.
Passage 2 is adapted from Angelina E. Grimké, *Letters to Catharine Beecher*. Originally published in 1838. Grimké encouraged Southern women to oppose slavery publicly.
Passage 1 is Beecher's response to Grimké's views.
Passage 2 is Grimké's response to Beecher.

Passage 1

Heaven has appointed to one sex the superior, and to the other the subordinate station, and this without any reference to the character or conduct of either. It is therefore as much for the dignity as it is for the interest of females, in all respects to conform to the duties of this relation. . . . But while woman holds a subordinate relation in society to the other sex, it is not because it was designed that her duties or her influence should be any the less important, or all-pervading. But it was designed that the mode of gaining influence and of exercising power should be altogether different and peculiar. . . .

A man may act on society by the collision of intellect, in public debate; he may urge his measures by a sense of shame, by fear and by personal interest; he may coerce by the combination of public sentiment; he may drive by physical force, and he does not outstep the boundaries of his sphere. But all the power, and all the conquests that are lawful to woman, are those only which appeal to the kindly, generous, peaceful and benevolent principles.

Woman is to win every thing by peace and love; by making herself so much respected, esteemed and loved, that to yield to her opinions and to gratify her wishes, will be the free-will offering of the heart. But this is to be all accomplished in the domestic and social circle. There let every woman become so cultivated and refined in intellect, that her taste and judgment will be respected; so benevolent in feeling and action; that her motives will be reverenced;—so unassuming and

302

unambitious, that collision and competition will be banished;—so "gentle and easy to be entreated," as that every heart will repose in her presence; then, the fathers, the husbands, and the sons, will find an influence thrown around them, to which they will yield not only willingly but proudly. . . .

A woman may seek the aid of co-operation and combination among her own sex, to assist her in her appropriate offices of piety, charity, maternal and domestic duty; but whatever, in any measure, throws a woman into the attitude of a combatant, either for herself or others—whatever binds her in a party conflict—whatever obliges her in any way to exert coercive influences, throws her out of her appropriate sphere. If these general principles are correct, they are entirely opposed to the plan of arraying females in any Abolition movement.

Passage 2

The investigation of the rights of the slave has led me to a better understanding of my own. I have found the Anti-Slavery cause to be the high school of morals in our land—the school in which human rights are more fully investigated, and better understood and taught, than in any other. Here a great fundamental principle is uplifted and illuminated, and from this central light, rays innumerable stream all around.

Human beings have rights, because they are moral beings: the rights of all men grow out of their moral nature; and as all men have the same moral nature, they have essentially the same rights. These rights may be wrested from the slave, but they cannot be alienated: his title to himself is as perfect now, as is that of Lyman Beecher:[1] it is stamped on his moral being, and is, like it, imperishable. Now if rights are founded in the nature of our moral being, then the mere *circumstance of sex* does not give to man higher rights and responsibilities, than to woman. To suppose that it does, would be to deny the self-evident truth, that the "physical constitution is the mere instrument of the moral nature." To suppose that it does, would be to break up utterly the relations, of the two natures, and to reverse their functions, exalting the animal nature into a monarch, and humbling the moral into a slave; making the former a proprietor, and the latter its property.

When human beings are regarded as moral beings, sex, instead of being enthroned upon the summit, administering upon rights and responsibilities, sinks into insignificance and nothingness. My doctrine then is, that whatever it is morally right for man to do, it is morally right for woman to do. Our duties originate, not from difference of sex, but from the diversity of our relations in life, the various gifts and talents committed to our care, and the different eras in which we live.

[1] Lyman Beecher was a famous minister and the father of Catharine Beecher.

Post-Passage Questions

1. Do your SRS for each passage!
2. Is the author of Passage 1 a man or a woman?

1. **Passage 1:** Beecher be like, "Women have a different role in society and they should stay inside of that role and not try to do the man's role."

   Passage 2: Grimké be like, "Men and women are equal, and they can do different things if they want."

2. She is a woman. Read the intro information!!

   This is important because we think of the past as just men thinking women were inferior. But, plenty of women also believed this and argued for the separation of gender roles and "spheres of influence". So, don't make assumptions!

Question 11

In Passage 1, Beecher makes which point about the status of women relative to that of men?

1. Women depend on men for their safety and security, but men are largely independent of women.
2. Women are inferior to men, but women play a role as significant as that played by men.
3. Women have fewer rights than men do, but women also have fewer responsibilities.
4. Women are superior to men, but tradition requires women to obey men.

Find your evidence!

Alright, it is time for a very big discussion. On the SAT, there will very often be a passage about women. It'll be about women's rights, women's suffrage, women's education, women's place in society (the SAT loves passages that talk about "spheres of influence" lol).

This type of passage comes up a lot, and…it's a trap! Look at all of these answer choices. They ALL sound like they could be true. Maybe not the first part of D (that's not a common narrative). But, the rest of it sounds totally reasonable!

That's my point. On these passages, the answers will always sound super reasonable and true of the world.

That. Is. Not. The. Point.

The point is that the answer be true OF THE PASSAGE. So, get out your magnifying glass and hyper focus on the words of the passage and NO outside knowledge (not for the women passages).

Also! Most of my male students get caught up in the idea of thinking "well, B is clearly wrong because women aren't inferior to men." I know that. You know that. But these passages are always going to have views from the past. In the past, people thought differently. So, don't get caught up in the ultimate truth of the answer choices. Just look at their relationship with the passage.

(Note: Most girls don't have this same issue, but you should still follow the same approach.)

Okay! The answer to this one is, in fact, B.

Best Evidence: "But while woman holds a subordinate relation in society to the other sex, it is not because it was designed that her duties or her influence should be any the less important, or all-pervading."

Question 13

In Passage 1, Beecher implies that women's effect on public life is largely

1. overlooked, because few men are interested in women's thoughts about politics.
2. indirect, because women exert their influence within the home and family life.
3. unnecessary, because men are able to govern society themselves.
4. symbolic, because women tend to be more idealistic about politics than men are.

Find your evidence!

I think students get this one wrong because of the whole issue of what we believe is true in real life. The narrative of the modern era is that women are still overlooked, especially in fields like business, engineering, politics, etc. But, that doesn't mean that's what Beecher thinks.

Maybe you picked unnecessary because it's sort of in line with women keeping to their own spheres. But, ask yourself what that would look like. Beecher would talk about how men are so successful at politics and governing that they just don't need any more help. That isn't conveyed here.

B is the correct answer. There is a common phrase in the world: "the neck that turns the head" The original was this: "The man may be the head of the household. But the woman is the neck, and she can turn the head whichever way she pleases."

Now, we know that our necks turn our heads, so hopefully you can understand what this is saying: Women are powerful; they have a certain amount of control.

Beecher's doesn't think that women should do manly things like, "coercing the public sentiment" (basically just arguing a bunch) or using "physical force" (like war and stuff). Beecher thinks that women should basically manipulate men with their "refined intellect" and "revered motives". Women are supposed to get men to yield "willingly" and "proudly" by being gentle, unassuming, unambitious…

All of that is indirect. It's done in the home, yet it can still have an impact in the broader world. Imagine if a woman is the wife of a judge or a politician. She could sway the way that he votes, or how he rules on a case, all through manipulation. That's a lot of power, but it's indirect. That's the whole point here.

Beecher isn't hating on women. She's just looking at things from a different perspective.

Best Evidence: "But this is to be all accomplished in the domestic and social circle."

Question 21

Beecher would most likely have reacted to lines 65-68 ("Now . . . woman") of Passage 2 with

    (A) sympathy, because she feels that human beings owe each other a debt to work together in the world.

    (B) agreement, because she feels that human responsibilities are a natural product of human rights.

    (C) dismay, because she feels that women actually have a more difficult role to play in society than men do.

    (D) disagreement, because she feels that the natures of men and women are fundamentally different.

I just add this one here to highlight how easy the SAT becomes when you have your SRS. Just knowing that Beecher thinks men and women have (and should have) different roles, and that Grimké disagrees, is enough to get D in a second. You can fly through questions like this!

Educating Women Dual Passage (Test 3)

Along with this passage, complete 4 MCAT passages.

You can take the full test 3 before reviewing these selected questions. I have included one other passage from test 3. It is the dual passages one, and it is the next passage after this.

For every question you get wrong on test 3, physically write down a clear explanation of why the answer you picked was wrong. Then, take another guess for the correct answer. (This requires that you always write your answers on a separate sheet and grade them simply by marking them right or wrong. That way you will know if the question is wrong, but you won't know the correct answer.)

If you get more than 2 questions wrong on the reading section of test 3, you should come see me: CSnyder@VohraMethod.com. If you get fewer than 2 wrong, then you're on track. Keep working!

Read this passage and do your ridiculous summary.

Passage 1 is adapted from Talleyrand et al., *Report on Public Instruction.* Originally published in 1791. Passage 2 is adapted from Mary Wollstonecraft, *A Vindication of the Rights of Woman.* Originally published in 1792. Talleyrand was a French diplomat; the Report was a plan for national education. Wollstonecraft, a British novelist and political writer, wrote Vindication in response to Talleyrand.

Passage 1

That half the human race is excluded by the other half from any participation in government; that they are native by birth but foreign by law in the very land where they were born; and that they are property-owners yet have no direct influence or representation: are all political phenomena apparently impossible to explain on abstract principle. But on another level of ideas, the question changes and may be easily resolved. The purpose of all these institutions must be the happiness of the greatest number. Everything that leads us farther from this purpose is in error; everything that brings us closer is truth. If the exclusion from public employments decreed against women leads to a greater sum of mutual happiness for the two sexes, then this becomes a law that all Societies have been compelled to acknowledge and sanction.

Any other ambition would be a reversal of our primary destinies; and it will never be in women's interest to change the assignment they have received.

It seems to us incontestable that our common happiness, above all that of women, requires that they never aspire to the exercise of political rights and functions. Here we must seek their interests in the wishes of nature. Is it not apparent, that their delicate constitutions, their peaceful inclinations, and the many duties of motherhood, set them apart from strenuous habits and onerous duties, and summon them to gentle occupations and the cares of the home? And is it not evident that the great conserving principle of Societies, which makes the division of powers a source of harmony, has been expressed and revealed by nature itself, when it divided the functions of the two sexes in so obviously distinct a manner? This is sufficient; we need not invoke principles that are inapplicable to the question. Let us not make rivals of life's companions. You must, you truly must allow the persistence of a union that no interest, no rivalry, can possibly undo. Understand that the good of all demands this of you.

Passage 2

Contending for the rights of woman, my main argument is built on this simple principle, that if she be not prepared by education to become the companion of man, she will stop the progress of knowledge and virtue; for truth must be common to all, or it will be inefficacious with respect to its influence on general practice. And how can woman be expected to co-operate unless she know why she ought to be virtuous? unless freedom strengthen her reason till she comprehend her duty, and see in what manner it is connected with her real good? If children are to be educated to understand the true principle of patriotism, their mother must be a patriot; and the love of mankind, from which an orderly train of virtues spring, can only be produced by considering the moral and civil interest of mankind; but the education and situation of woman, at present, shuts her out from such investigations. . . .

Consider, sir, dispassionately, these observations—for a glimpse of this truth seemed to open before you when you observed, "that to see one half of the human race excluded by the other from all participation of government, was a political phenomenon that, according to abstract principles, it was impossible to explain." If so, on what does your constitution rest? If the abstract rights of man will bear discussion and explanation, those of woman, by a parity of reasoning, will not shrink from the same test: though a different opinion prevails in this country, built on the very arguments which you use to justify the oppression of woman—prescription.

Consider—I address you as a legislator— whether, when men contend for their freedom, and to be allowed to judge for themselves respecting their own happiness, it be not inconsistent and unjust to subjugate women, even though you firmly believe that you are acting in the manner best calculated to promote their happiness? Who made man the exclusive judge, if woman partake with him the gift of reason?

In this style, argue tyrants of every denomination , from the weak king to the weak father of a family; they are all eager to crush reason; yet always assert that they usurp its throne only to be useful. Do you not act a similar part, when you force all women, by denying them civil and political rights, to remain immured in their families groping in the dark?

Post-Passage Question

1. Do your SRS for both passages!

1. **Passage 1:** Basically the standard story. Talleyrand be like, "Women shouldn't vote or leave the home because everyone will be happier if they don't, including women!"

    Passage 2: Again the standard story: Wollstonecraft be like, "Women should be allowed to learn stuff and decide what's best for themselves."

    Now, just because this feels like the standard pro-women vs anti-women argument **doesn't mean** that you should turn your brain off and pick answers that don't relate to what the passages actually say. Don't be dumb.

Question 32

It can be inferred that the authors of Passage 1 believe that running a household and raising children

- **(A)** are rewarding for men as well as for women.
- **(B)** yield less value for society than do the roles performed by men.
- **(C)** entail very few activities that are difficult or unpleasant.
- **(D)** require skills similar to those needed to run a country or a business.

Find your evidence!

A is sometimes true today but it's not at all what the passage is saying! (Everybody likes to pick it though. Don't fall into the same traps!)

B is part of the standard trope of "women aren't as good as men". But! That's not what this passage is saying. Passage 1 says that the way they have society set up "makes the division of powers a source of harmony". He also talks about the greater happiness of everyone, women AND men. Meaning, the greatest value to society is obtained when women stay home and men do the politics.

C is the correct answer.

Best Evidence: "Is it not apparent, that their **delicate** constitutions, their **peaceful** inclinations, and the many duties of motherhood, **set them apart from strenuous habits and onerous duties**, and summon them to **gentle occupations and the cares of the home?**"

This is talking about how the home is not as difficult or unpleasant.

Most students don't pick D. The above evidence would be equally good at disproving D, as Talleyrand is explaining the clear differences between the home life and the life of business or politics.

Question 34

According to the author of Passage 2, in order for society to progress, women must

    (A) enjoy personal happiness and financial security.

    (B) follow all currently prescribed social rules.

    (C) replace men as figures of power and authority.

    (D) receive an education comparable to that of men.

Find your evidence!

Most students don't pick B; that would be more in line with the first passage.

Many students pick A or C. If you did, then you're still thinking of this argument in a modern context. Don't bring the modern era into it. Don't bring ANYthing into it. Focus only on what the passages clearly state. Passage 2 never advocates for women replacing men in politics, nor does she advocate financial independence or anything of the sort.

She does, however, talk about how important it is that women be educated so they can become good patriots and advance society. So, the answer is D.

Best Evidence: "…if she be not prepared by education to become the companion of man, she will stop the progress of knowledge and virtue"

Abraham Lincoln vs Thoreau (Test 6)

Along with this passage, complete 4 MCAT passages.

You can take the full test 6 before reviewing these selected questions. I have included one other passage from test 6. It is the fictional Nawabdin passage (above).

For every question you get wrong on test 6, physically write down a clear explanation of why the answer you picked was wrong. Then, take another guess for the correct answer. (This requires that you always write your answers on a separate sheet and grade them simply by marking them right or wrong. That way you will know if the question is wrong, but you won't know the correct answer.)

If you get more than 8 questions wrong on the reading section of test 6, you should come see me: CSnyder@VohraMethod.com. If you get fewer than 8 wrong, then you're on track. Keep working!

Experiment: On this test, you'll practice your SAT intuition. You do not have to take this test timed.

SAT intuition is that magical thing that students are always referring to called "test taking ability" or something similar. It's not magic; it turns out. It's just logic. Here's how you practice:

For all NON-fiction passages, DO NOT read the passage. You can read **just** the passage intro information to know the general topic. Then, read through the questions (skip the words in context ones and the evidence ones) and look for any answer choices that are either highly likely or highly unlikely without ever having read the passage.

You'll find that there are plenty of answer choices that are just almost certainly not the answer, unless the passage takes some big and very obvious and unexpected turn... You'll find that there are some answer choices that are very probably right just given what you know about the context of the discussion surrounding women throughout history, or the way that the scientific method works (hypothesis, test, conclusion...for the most part).

And you'll find that sometimes, a full THREE answer choices are very, very unlikely, and ONE seems quite likely. Meaning, sometimes you can get the answer from logic and general world knowledge alone, without having read the passage at all.

On the real test, you'll read the passage and then answer the questions. But, you will have practiced this skill of looking plainly at what is likely or unlikely based on general knowledge, so you won't get tricked by answer choices that are wildly weird but just happen to contain a few memorable words from the passage.

Sometimes, you'll end up with just two that are unlikely, and two answer choices that are possible candidates. This can help you to see the difference between a logical answer and…**a logical answer that is actually supported by the passage.** That's a critical differentiation!

Again, try this for the science and history passages, not for the fiction. Fiction is all made up, so you can't really "logic" your way through it.

Side note: It's kind of epic that Lincoln encouraged people to "swear by the blood of the Revolution". That's intense! Imagine what that time was like…overthrowing a tyrannical government, making a new one from scratch (pretty much), everything brand new…

Read this passage and do your ridiculous summary. Then, we'll see if you understood the crux of this passage with a couple of questions!

Passage 1 is adapted from Abraham Lincoln, *"Address to the Young Men's Lyceum of Springfield, Illinois."* Originally delivered in 1838. Passage 2 is from Henry David Thoreau, "Resistance to Civil Government." Originally published in 1849.

Passage 1

Let every American, every lover of liberty, every well wisher to his posterity, swear by the blood of the Revolution, never to violate in the least particular, the laws of the country; and never to tolerate their violation by others. As the patriots of seventy-six did to the support of the Declaration of Independence, so to the support of the Constitution and Laws, let every American pledge his life, his property, and his sacred honor;—let every man remember that to violate the law, is to trample on the blood of his father, and to tear the character of his own, and his children's liberty. Let reverence for the laws, be breathed by every American mother, to the lisping babe, that prattles on her lap—let it be taught in schools, in seminaries, and in colleges;—let it be written in Primers, spelling books, and in Almanacs;—let it be preached from the pulpit, proclaimed in legislative halls, and enforced in courts of justice. And, in short, let it become the political religion of the nation; and let the old and the young, the rich and the poor, the grave and the gay, of all sexes and tongues, and colors and conditions, sacrifice unceasingly upon its altars. . . .

When I so pressingly urge a strict observance of all the laws, let me not be understood as saying there are no bad laws, nor that grievances may not arise, for the redress of which, no legal provisions have been made. I mean to say no such thing. But I do mean to say, that, although bad laws, if they exist, should be repealed as soon as possible, still while they continue in force, for the sake of example, they should be religiously observed. So also in unprovided cases. If such arise, let proper legal provisions be made for them with the least possible delay; but, till then, let them if not too intolerable, be borne with.

There is no grievance that is a fit object of redress by mob law. In any case that arises, as for instance, the promulgation of abolitionism, one of two positions is necessarily true; that is, the thing is right within itself, and therefore deserves the protection of all law and all good citizens; or, it is wrong, and therefore proper to be prohibited by legal enactments; and in neither case, is the interposition of mob law, either necessary, justifiable, or excusable.

Passage 2

Unjust laws exist; shall we be content to obey them, or shall we endeavor to amend them, and obey them until we have succeeded, or shall we transgress them at once? Men generally, under such a government as this, think that they ought to wait until they have persuaded the majority to alter them. They think that, if they should resist, the remedy would be worse than the evil. But it is the fault of the government itself that the remedy is worse than the evil. It makes it worse. Why is it not more apt to anticipate and provide for reform? Why does it not cherish its wise minority? Why does it cry and resist before it is hurt? . . .

If the injustice is part of the necessary friction of the machine of government, let it go, let it go; perchance it will wear smooth—certainly the machine will wear out. If the injustice has a spring, or a pulley, or a rope, or a crank, exclusively for itself, then perhaps you may consider whether the remedy will not be worse than the evil; but if it is of such a nature that it requires you to be the agent of injustice to another, then, I say, break the law. Let your life be a counter friction to stop the machine. What I have to do is to see, at any rate, that I do not lend myself to the wrong which I condemn.

As for adopting the ways which the State has provided for remedying the evil, I know not of such ways. They take too much time, and a man's life will be gone. I have other affairs to attend to. I came into this world, not chiefly to make this a good place to live in, but to live in it, be it good or bad. A man has not everything to do, but something; and because he cannot do everything, it is not necessary that he should do something wrong. . . .

I do not hesitate to say, that those who call themselves Abolitionists should at once effectually withdraw their support, both in person and property, from the government . . . and not wait till they constitute a majority of one, before they suffer the right to prevail through them. I think that it is enough if they have God on their side, without waiting for that other one. Moreover, any man more right than his neighbors constitutes a majority of one already.

Post-Passage Questions

1. Do your SRS.
2. What is "mob law"?
3. Are Lincoln and Thoreau abolitionists? How do you know? Evidence!

1. **Passage 1:** Lincoln be like, "People should follow the law. Seriously, really really follow it. For realz."
   Passage 2: Thoreau be like, "If a law is bad, don't follow it. That would be dumb."

2. Lincoln isn't talking about an actual mob getting together with pitchforks and stuff. What this means is basically the common man deciding what's best, and then acting on it. The "mob" of people in a city, state, or even country creating the law. Obviously, most politicians didn't really want the mob creating the law. Also, most common people probably don't want mob law, just in case the mob suddenly decides that…stealing is okay! Or anything like that.

   Here, Lincoln is stressing the point that people should follow the law as it is written and created by the government. Don't make your own laws. Don't break the laws. Worship the laws the government created, yada yada. All that.

3. Neither of them are, no.

   We can be pretty sure Lincoln isn't because he presents the case for Abolitionism by saying "either it's right or it's wrong". Not exactly a huge sign of membership, there.

   For Thoreau, here's a useful trick: look at his pronouns. He calls them, "those who call themselves Abolitionists" and goes on to refer to them as "they" a lot. That's distancing language. If he felt like he was a part of them, he would say "we".

   This trick comes in handy pretty often for determining if someone believes something personally or is just discussing it in the abstract or in the context of others.

Question 38

In Passage 2, Thoreau indicates that some unjust aspects of government are

   (A) superficial and can be fixed easily.
   (B) subtle and must be studied carefully.
   (C) self-correcting and may be beneficial.
   (D) inevitable and should be endured.

Find your evidence!

Yowza. This one is pretty tough. It goes completely against the SRS (superficially). It is also supported by a pretty tough piece of evidence.

Evidence: "If the injustice is part of the necessary friction of the machine of government, let it go, let it go…"

What is "the necessary friction of the government"? What exactly does "let it go" mean?

If you missed this question, you really should just get a bunch of texts from this time period and read them all. They're largely going to be free and accessible online. Just get practice with reading language and structure like this.

Thoreau is saying that if some particular bad thing is a necessary evil for doing good, then don't worry about it. Let it be.

This goes along with his point later that he came into this world to live, not just to make it more perfect. It's his job to do SOMEthing with his life, but he doesn't have to fix EVERYthing. Sometimes, you can just let things be and endure.

Answer is D.

Question 42

Based on the passages, one commonality in the stances Lincoln and Thoreau take toward abolitionism is that

   (A) both authors see the cause as warranting drastic action.
   (B) both authors view the cause as central to their argument.
   (C) neither author expects the cause to win widespread acceptance.
   (D) neither author embraces the cause as his own.

This is a pretty common thing. In the dual passages, the authors will be talking about some main topic, and then they'll each bring in a **side topic** towards the end or briefly in the middle. The side topic, whatever it is, will almost always account for one question on your test. So, just be sure to think about how each author feels about the side topic (in addition to the main topic!).

Answer is D. We discussed this in the post-passage questions.

Appendix A: Advice

In this section, I'll address some of the most common questions my students ask about studying for the SAT and performing well on test day.

Resting the Brain & "Accurate" Preparation

A lot of students come to me with questions like this:

> » Should I intentionally not do any studying the day before the test?
> » Should I do some practice tests early in the morning on a Saturday (around the same time as the real test)?
> » Do I have to take full 4-hour practice tests all at once?
> » Should I change my sleep schedule so I can get used to waking up early in the morning?
> » What do I do if I'm tired on the day of the test?

To all questions of this type, I have one clear response: **You never forget English**.

If I woke you up in the middle of the night and asked you to read a book aloud, you could do it. You might be groggy for the first few minutes, but you wouldn't suddenly forget all the words.

If you stayed up all night long with no sleep, and I handed you a test on basic addition in the morning, you could do it. You would almost certainly be tired, but you wouldn't forget that 2+2=4.

That's what real knowledge is. When you KNOW something, you know it. You know your mom's name. You know how old you are. You know that that thing with four legs and a floofy tail that bounding at you with love is called a "dog". You don't really forget things that you KNOW.

Student: But Chelsey, I don't KNOW advanced Calculus.

Me: Good point, dear student. If you don't know something so well that you could do it when groggy or really hungry or cold or whatever...then you don't KNOW that thing. For the SAT, you need to KNOW your grammar, KNOW your reading, and KNOW your algebra.

If you KNOW those things, you'll be fine. If you don't KNOW those things, then no amount of extra sleep is going to help you. No altered sleep schedule, no amount of mental rest will make the difference.

That said, **here are a few things I do recommend**:

» When taking practice tests, **do whatever practice you can in the time that you have**. If you have time for just one section of math, do that. If you have time for the full Verbal section (reading & grammar), then do that. If you can make the time for a full test, do that. Just practice. Don't not practice. And definitely don't hold out until you can get that "perfect" study session into your busy schedule. Life isn't about perfect. Life is about showing up.

» **Obviously, get good sleep the night before!** You should get good sleep as many nights of your life as you possibly can. Good sleep is just so obviously necessary for brain development, healing, memory storage, bodily health, emotional health, and a billion other aspects of your life. So yes, get good sleep the night before and all other nights forever.

» If you're worried about waking up, **plan a quick workout**. Just some push ups, jumping jacks, bodyweight squats, whatever. You don't have to go crazy here. But, working out and getting your blood flowing is, in my experience, the best way to wake up your brain and clear the fog.

» **Don't start experimenting with coffee and energy drinks, and don't create brand new life schedules right now.** Now is not the time to introduce new variables into your routine. Just stick with what you know.

» **Keep doing your Vocab Synapse.** Remember, on test day, you can "logic" your way through a lot of reading questions. You can ask yourself what different things would look like. You can try to disprove based on individual words. You can think about whether an answer choice is likely or unlikely. But! you cannot "logic" your way through a word you simply don't know. One day of Vocab Synapse training could be the difference between a 1490 and a 1500, or a 1530 and a 1550. At worst, you learned a few more words. At best, you bought yourself 10-20+ extra points on the SAT. It's a no-brainer.

» **On the day before your test, keep studying...or don't.** If you've gotten through a lot of the suggested material in this book, then take a day off. If you haven't, then maybe keep studying. But, you really, mostly only need a few things. Your SRS. Disprove; Don't Prove. Disprove using a single word. Disprove by asking yourself, "What would it look like if A/B/C/D were true?". And vocabulary. You don't need a million tools; you just need to use the few tools you have. Once you have those tools and you're automatically relying on them in practice tests, you're good.

Test Day

The questions here are usually something like this:

> » What do I do if I don't know something on the actual test?
> » What do I do if I get really anxious and doubt myself on test day?
> » What do I do if I don't know a word on the actual test?

The general answer is this: On test day, you know what you know. There is absolutely nothing you can do to magically know more than you know while you are taking a closed-book, monitored exam. So, your job is to learn as much as you possibly can before that day. Plain and simple.

I'll give a few more details on each of these questions, though.

If you don't understand a particular part of a passage, just ignore it and hope really hard that it's not important for any of the questions.

That might sound like weird advice, but I want to dive into the options here. So, there's a bit in the passage that you don't understand. Either that bit is important, or it isn't. Not every bit in a passage gets turned into a question, after all.

Let's say this particular bit isn't important. Then, if you worry, you just got all wound up for nothing. You might even get a question wrong that you would otherwise have gotten right, all because you were worried that you missed something, and so you started to doubt yourself and do some Mental Gymnastics. That would be very silly.

Or, let's say this particular bit is important; it does show up in at least one question. Again, worrying won't make any difference at all. Worry doesn't know the right answer. Worry doesn't think clearly.

Either way, worrying won't help you. So, just hope the confusing bit isn't important and don't sweat it.

That said, you know what I do recommend?

> » Use your SRS!
> » Disprove; Don't Prove.
> » Disprove using a single word.
> » Disprove by asking yourself, "What would it look like if…?"
> » Use logic.

If you really commit to those tools, you can still get a lot of questions right, even when you don't understand bits of the passage. The whole point of the SRS is to help you get the big ideas of the passage, even if the little ideas elude you. The whole point of all the disproving tactics is to help you critically analyze the question text and the answer choices, even if you're not 100% sure what everything says. And sometimes you can disprove 3 out of 4 answer choices simply by thinking about what is likely or unlikely to be the answer with relatively little input from the passages at all.

When you're really stuck or lost in a passage, I want you to lean more heavily into the What would it look like if… skill. This saves students quite often. Even if you don't know exactly what the passage IS doing, you might be able to notice that it clearly is NOT doing whatever answer choice B says. And now your chances of getting the answer correct just went up. Disprove one more answer choice and you're at 50/50. Keep going and you can answer questions solely by **confidently** disproving answer choices that are obviously wrong.

And remember, don't worry. Even if this is the last possible test you can take, worrying won't help you. Worrying will never help you accomplish anything in your life ever. So, don't do it.

If you start experiencing emotions during the test, turn them off! If you start to feel anxious, if you start to doubt yourself, if you start to worry, if you get afraid that you're moving too slowly or making a lot of mistakes...turn it all off.

I already explained that emotions won't help you, but how do you just get rid of them?

I like to imagine myself just smacking myself in the face and shouting, "Snap out of it!". Or, I imagine myself pouring a bucket of super cold water on my head.

You can't actually do either of those things on testing day, but you can still imagine them. You can also conjure an image of me yelling at you not to panic, if that helps. You can think of a funny joke, or a really bad dad joke that you just can't help laughing at.

The bottom line is you need to distract yourself and get back on the right track. So, imagine something goofy or something shocking, I don't care. Just snap yourself out of it.

And here's the cheesy part...

Believe in yourself and the work you've done. If you didn't do everything in this book, then maybe you're not 100% ready. But, maybe you can still get a really high score. The whole point of this book is to accomplish more with just a little bit of prep. So, just believe in your new skills. Believe in the things I told you you all are always really good at. Believe in the process of disproving. Actually DO your disproving. DO your Simple Ridiculous Summary. DO your logic and your What would it look like if... Use the skills you've learned, and believe that they are enough. Lean into them. Rely on them.

When students come to me on their 5th or 6th or 7th practice test and they're still getting a lot of questions wrong, it's always because they haven't yet fully committed to using the skills this book has taught. They still aren't really doing the SRS. They aren't asking themselves What would it look like if... They aren't focusing on disproving or logic or likely vs unlikely.

I give them a lecture. They go take another test. And their number of wrong questions decreases dramatically. It's not magic; it's clear and functional tactics that you have to USE fo them to help you.

I believe that is the end of my lecture to you. Don't make me have to give you this lecture again after you take the real test. Just use your new skills on the real test and crush it. No worry or anxiety required.

If you don't know a word on the test, again you just hope really hard that it's not important. There's not much new here, but I will take one extra moment to say that studying your vocabulary is important.

You can use flashcards if you want. You can use other online programs. You can use our Vocab Synapse program. I don't care. But you should study vocabulary every day from the day you start reading this book until the day of your test.

You cannot guess your way through vocabulary. The SAT will use words that sort of sound like they have a positive connotation, when they are actually negative (or vice versa). Their primary goal is to trick you, obviously.

That said, if there's a word that you don't know in any passage, question, or answer choice...just ignore it and hope it's not important. What else can you do?

Still use your skills. Let's say answer choice B has a word you don't know. Skip that one at first; get to it last. If you can disprove every other answer choice, then maybe B is the right one. But, if you have a really hard time disproving D, and you find evidence that you think supports D, then pick D. Don't just pick B because you don't understand it and so you're worried it might be right.

Ignore answer choices with unfamiliar words and hope that they're wrong until you have clearly and firmly disproved every other option. Pick the unfamiliar answer choice as a last resort.

This process works MOST of the time, by the way. If your disproving is strong, then you'll disprove all other options and you'll only have the one left. If you can't disprove some other option, then pick that one, not the one you don't understand!

And that's it. On test day, you know what you know and nothing more. So, use what you know, and **do your Vocab Synapse!**

Getting a High Enough Score

So many students ask me some variation of the question, "What do I do if I don't get a high enough score?"

I'll be honest, this question does confuse me a little. Personally, I'm a very stubborn individual. If I don't get what I want, I'm going to keep trying to get it...until I get it. If I want a perfect score, I'll take the test as many times as it takes to get that perfect score. (And no, colleges won't judge you poorly if you took the test several times and continued to **improve** your score. That just shows hard work, diligence, personal desire to improve and grow, etc.)

So, that's what I would do. That's also what I'll tell you to do.

Yes, I know, you don't WANT to take it more than once. You don't want to take it at all, probably. But you probably do want to get into some particular college that has some particular SAT score minimum or average or whatever. So, keep working until you get the score you need. It's that simple.

There is no magic here. It's just hard work, real learning, and very empowering success.

Appendix B: Your Pre-Test Cheat Sheet

DO NOT look at this during your practice tests. This is a PRE-TEST cheat sheet, not a DURING test cheat sheet, obviously.

Feel free to rip these pages out of this book and carry them with you to your real test!

1. **The SRS – Use it!**

2. **FOCUS**
   Focus on actions in Fiction.
   Focus on opinions in Science.
   Focus on disagreements in Dual Passages.
   Focus on grammar in History.

3. **Disprove; Don't Prove.**
   Disprove using a single word.
   Disprove by asking, "What would _________ look like?"

4. **DO NOT answer the question + evidence pair together.**
   Make sure your evidence actually proves the answer choice you picked.

5. **DO NOT** cherry pick single words out of the passage, ignoring their context, and then blindly pick an answer!
   Don't let the SAT take things out of context and trick you.

6. Use what you already know!

7. Don't project your own emotions into the characters in the story.

8. Don't do Mental Gymnastics.

9. Ask yourself questions in order to force your brain to engage with these (let's be honest) sometimes kinda boring passages.

10. Read the introductory information above every passage. Do not make me laugh at you!

11. Look for places where two vague "characters" are introduced very close together. Make sure you differentiate the details about them

12. Look for places where the passage is VERY close to what the question says. It will often be nearly word for word identical. Then, you know that's where you should be looking for evidence.

13. Don't cross off an answer choice just because you don't "get it"

14. For vocab questions, look for the contextual match, not just a definitional match.

15. For tone: NOT EVERYTHING CAN BE SCIENTIFIC AND INFORMATIVE

16. Think about the severity of words, opinions, emotions, anything.

17. Know the definition of "ambivalent"! The SAT loves this word.

18. Make note of big changes in a passage. Some new thing introduced at paragraph 4. A discussion that shifts from before event X to after event X. A strong tonal shift.

19. In historical passages, "should" often means "would". The way they used to use the word "should" is equivalent to our modern word "would".
Noun clauses starting with "that" can often be replace with "the fact that" to make it easier to read.

20. Unsure about main purpose? Literally just count the sentences/paragraphs/whatever pertaining to each answer choice. Main purpose means it should take up more physical real estate on the page!

21. Pay attention to what data in a graph **can actually, possibly prove.**

22. For questions about the graph, disprove as many answer choices as you can by looking at the graph ONLY, first. Then, if you still have two options left, go into the passage for further evidence.

23. Ask yourself, "Are there any limitations in this scientific study?"

24. Look for distancing language like "they/them" and "that". If someone feels a part of something, they'll usually say "we", not "them". Or they'll say "this", not "that".

25. Look out for side topics in dual passages. Often, the authors will be discussing one main thing, and then both will briefly mention a smaller issue. The smaller issue will almost certainly account for 1-2 questions.

Appendix C: SAT Reading Book List

Beowulf

Things Fall Apart by Chinua Achebe

A Death in the Family by James Agee

Pride and Prejudice by Jane Austen

Go Tell It on the Mountain by James Baldwin

Waiting for Godot by Samuel Beckett

The Adventures of Augie March by Saul Bellow

Jane Eyre by Charlotte Brontë

Wuthering Heights by Emily Brontë

The Stranger by Albert Camus

Death Comes for the Archbishop by Willa Cather

The Canterbury Tales by Geoffrey Chaucer

The Cherry Orchard by Anton Chekhov

The Awakening by Kate Chopin

Heart of Darkness by Joseph Conrad

Fenimore The Last of the Mohicans by James Cooper

The Red Badge of Courage by Stephen Crane

Inferno by Dante

Don Quixote by Miguel de Cervantes

Robinson Crusoe by Daniel Defoe

A Tale of Two Cities by Charles Dickens

Crime and Punishment by Fyodor Dostoyevsky

Narrative of the Life of Frederick Douglass by Frederick Douglass

An American Tragedy by Theodore Dreiser

The Three Musketeers by Alexandre Dumas

The Mill on the Floss by George Eliot

Invisible Man by Ralph Ellison

Waldo Selected Essays by Ralph Emerson

As I Lay Dying by William Faulkner

The Sound and the Fury by William Faulkner

Tom Jones by Henry Fielding

The Great Gatsby by F. Scott Fitzgerald

Madame Bovary by Gustave Flaubert

The Good Soldier by Ford Madox Ford

Wolfgang von Faust by Johann Goethe

Lord of the Flies by William Golding

Tess of the d'Urbervilles by Thomas Hardy

The Scarlet Letter by Nathanial Hawthorne

Catch-22 by Joseph Heller

A Farewell to Arms by Ernest Hemingway

The Iliad by Homer

The Odyssey by Homer

The Hunchback of Notre Dame by Victor Hugo

Their Eyes Were Watching God by Zora Neale Hurston

Brave New World by Aldous Huxley

A Doll's House by Henrik Ibsen

The Portrait of a Lady by Henry James

The Turn of the Screw by Henry James

A Portrait of the Artist as a Young Man by James Joyce

The Metamorphosis by Franz Kafka

Hong The Woman Warrior by Maxine Kingston

To Kill a Mockingbird by Harper Lee

Babbitt by Sinclair Lewis

The Call of the Wild by Jack London

The Magic Mountain by Thomas Mann

García One Hundred Years of Solitude by Gabriel Marquez

Bartleby the Scrivener by Herman Melville

Moby Dick by Herman Melville

The Crucible by Arthur Miller

Beloved by Toni Morrison

A Good Man Is Hard to Find by Flannery O'Connor

Long Day's Journey into Night by Eugene O'Neill

Animal Farm by George Orwell

Doctor Zhivago by Boris Pasternak

The Bell Jar by Sylvia Plath

Allan Selected Tales by Edgar Poe

Swann's Way by Marcel Proust

The Crying of Lot 49 by Thomas Pynchon

Maria All Quiet on the Western Front by Erich Remarque

Cyrano de Bergerac by Edmond Rostand

Call It Sleep by Henry Roth

The Catcher in the Rye by J.D. Salinger

Hamlet by William Shakespeare

Macbeth by William Shakespeare

A Midsummer Night's Dream by William Shakespeare

Romeo and Juliet by William Shakespeare

Pygmalion by George Bernard Shaw

Frankenstein by Mary Shelley

Marmon Ceremony by Leslie Silko

One Day in the Life of Ivan Denisovich by Alexander Solzhenitsyn

Antigone by Sophocles

Oedipus Rex by Sophocles

The Grapes of Wrath by John Steinbeck

Louis Treasure Island by Robert Stevenson

Beecher Uncle Tom's Cabin by Harriet Stowe

Gulliver's Travels by Jonathan Swift

Vanity Fair by William Thackeray

Walden by Henry David Thoreau

War and Peace by Leo Tolstoy

Fathers and Sons by Ivan Turgenev

The Adventures of Huckleberry Finn by Mark Twain

Candide by Voltaire

Jr. Slaughterhouse-Five by Kurt Vonnegut

The Color Purple by Alice Walker

The House of Mirth by Edith Wharton

Collected Stories by Eudora Welty

Leaves of Grass by Walt Whitman

The Picture of Dorian Gray by Oscar Wilde

The Glass Menagerie by Tennessee Williams

To the Lighthouse by Virginia Woolf

Native Son by Richard Wright

www.ingramcontent.com/pod-product-compliance
Lightning Source LLC
Chambersburg PA
CBHW051649031125
34902CB00048B/928